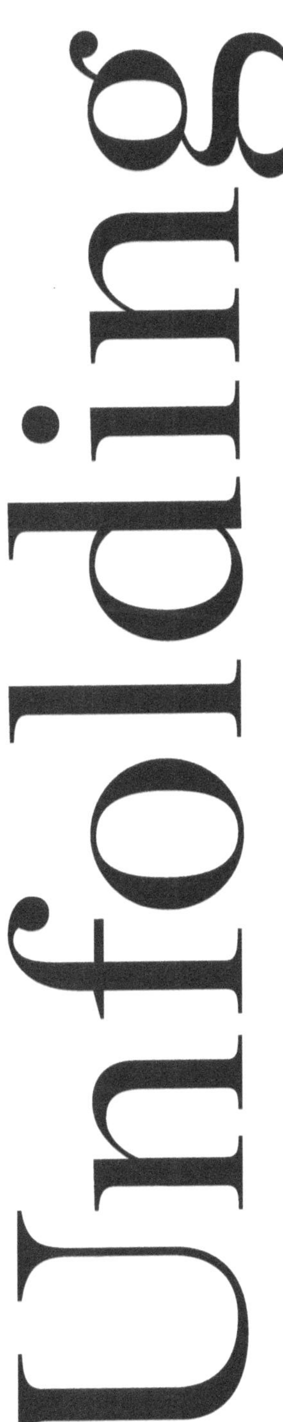

Unfolding

A
MARKET
STREET
WRITERS
ANTHOLOGY

Edited by
LISA COLBURN

I hear the singing of the lives of women ...
MURIEL RUKEYSER

Contents

Herstory

Writing

Longings

Reverence

Introduction

A women's writing circle holds great power. As I watch the women in my living room or on Zoom, heads bent over notebooks, pens scratching furiously, I see stories being born. I see women unlocking their voices, allowing memories to unspool, and new characters emerging as if by magic. And imagination *is* a sort of magic, isn't it? We create worlds with our words. We come to know ourselves more deeply. Then, as we share our stories and listen to one another without judgment, something in us loosens and shifts. We are changed.

The book you hold in your hands celebrates women's voices. In the twelve years I have led writing workshops and retreats, more than three hundred women (and a few men) have written with me and read their new stories and poems aloud. It was a privilege to witness each one. Now I want to pull back the curtain so that you, too, can see the power of the writing circle; so that you, too, can discover in these stories and poems the thread that connects us all—our common humanity, in all our strength and frailty, our darkness and our light.

We are made of stories, as surely as we are made of blood and bone. From the time the first distant ancestor leaned toward the fire and told those gathered there of the hunt, we have connected with each other through storytelling. We have taught, entertained, and expressed our deepest truths. And while the means of delivery and much of the subject matter has changed, our DNA has not. We are human. We are story.

For this anthology I invited everyone who had ever participated in a Market Street Writers workshop or retreat to submit their work. Forty-two women took me up on my offer, and each has at least one poem, essay, or piece of short fiction included. Here you will find writing from those who have published widely and others who are seeing their creative writing in print for the first time. We have professors and authors, teachers and social workers, artists and entrepreneurs, government workers and scientists—and even a shamanic practitioner! For each one, writing is part of her creative path. I am proud of the work they have shared.

Welcoming people at all levels of experience to the writing circle is a core principle of the late Pat Schneider, founder of the Amherst Writers & Artists (AWA) method I use in my workshops. Pat had "Five Essential Affirmations," which can be found in her book *Writing Alone and with Others* (Oxford University Press, 2003):

1. Everyone has a strong, unique voice.
2. Everyone is born with creative genius.
3. Writing as an art form belongs to all people, regardless of economic class or educational level.
4. The teaching of craft can be done without damage to a writer's original voice or artistic self-esteem.
5. A writer is someone who writes.

This underpinning of egalitarianism, generosity, welcome, and celebration is a precious and often rare gift in writing workshops. I first experienced the power of the AWA method when I participated in Maggie Butler's "In Your Write Mind" retreat in Capon Springs, West Virginia, in 2009. Maggie, a gifted leader, challenged us with exciting writing prompts and encouraged us to read our work aloud and support each other with only positive feedback—a practice I had not previously encountered.

The retreat was a revelation. Sitting in a circle of fifteen women on a glorious October weekend, I rediscovered my love of writing. Finally, after twenty years as an editor, I wasn't drilling down into a manuscript to search out its flaws, nor was I managing the myriad moving parts of a magazine. Instead, I was a kid in a sandbox, filled with the sheer joy of creation. My imagination ignited with each new writing prompt. I wrote until my hand cramped, great loops of words scrawled into my notebook. I wrote about my mother's 1970s avocado kitchen, my Scots-Irish ancestors, the agonies of being a tall girl in junior high, and much more. Everything poured out of me—short stories, poems, memories—and it felt good and true, like cold, clear mountain water. I read my new work aloud, even as my voice shook a little. Something in me broke free, soared. I was hooked.

A few years later, in April 2012, I traveled to Pat Schneider's charming yellow farmhouse in Amherst, Massachusetts, to be trained as a writing workshop leader. It was there that I learned how to find good writing prompts and to create sacred space for new stories and poems to emerge, fresh and bold as the first daffodils of spring. And although I couldn't know it at the time, it was there that the seeds for this anthology were planted.

Unfolding has five broad themes:

In "Origins," we read about the prehistoric earth, ancestral influences, and childhood memories. These include a touching elementary school art lesson, a milestone bus ride, and a response to a classic AWA writing prompt: "Where I'm From" by George Ella Lyon.

"Herstory" features romantic and familial relationships, journeys to independence, aging, and what it means to go through life in a female body. We read about significant objects—record albums, couches, reading glasses, bicycles—and a tour boat experience that goes terribly wrong.

"Writing" covers resistance, procrastination, and wrestling with words, but also the wonder and magic of creating. We learn about the reassurance of holding a Dixon Ticonderoga #2 pencil, a library that offers more than books, and how poems can get downright sassy.

"Longings" encompasses the desire for romantic love, as well as a polar bear's hunger for a place to rest, a woman's craving for a body free from illness, the universal yearning for a place to call home, and the remembrance of loved ones no longer with us.

"Reverence" finds the miraculous in a spider's web and an ant on the rim of a cat's water bowl. We also enter the spiritual realm, exploring death and what lies beyond it. We end with "Unfolding," which invites us to immerse ourselves in the natural world, awakening a sense of possibility, even hope.

In the Appendix, you will find a list of writing prompts for the stories and poems that had their origins in writing workshops.

Today I feel the same sense of mysterious alchemy, the same wonder and joy, that I had when I began leading workshops twelve years ago. I love the element of surprise in a new writing prompt, to see writers roll it around in their minds and find out where it lives in their bodies. What memories will it stir? What sparks of imagination will roar to flame? I love, too, how writing together in a circle of mutual support lifts us to new creative heights, challenging us to take greater risks and to excavate and express our truth.

Many of you reading this have sat in a writer's circle with me. I am grateful for your companionship on the writing journey, as well as the welcoming community we have co-created. I celebrate the stories and poems you have shared. It was a joy to witness their birth, and I honor the wisdom, power, and emotion they carry. May our circle ever expand to include new voices, new stories.

Lisa Colburn
Founder, Market Street Writers
Leesburg, Virginia

Origins

Gulf Coast Morning

BARBARA FARMER

after "Soft Thunder" by Jake Skeets

The Sun knows best when it rises,
as sea fog smothers morning

with mist like soft tendrils,
caressing the sky.

A tiny glimpse of brightness peeks through
as morning hours grow.

Fog lifts, exposes green
thick St. Augustine grass.

Dew melts on palms
as stillness awakens.

Fog lifts higher and higher,
a soft glow and glimmer

as the Sun opens selfishly,
takes over the day.

Before the People Came

BARBARA GALVIN

after "The Theft Outright" by Heid E. Erdrich

We were the land before we were people.
Created from nothing into dirt and clay,
molded into mountains, deserts,
and wind-whipped valleys.

We were the land before we were people.
Barren stretches unnoticed,
hills unclimbed, deserts untouched,
vast, sunbaked, parched.

We were the land before we were people.
Then rain came, carving rivers,
flowing downstream to oceans,
drenching the scorched earth.

We were the land before we were people.
Now lush with forests,
trees touching the skies,
swallowing the stars.

We were the land before we were people.
Earth, wind, and sky
in symbiotic balance,
existing in tranquility.

Then the people came,
polluting our waters,
gouging our earth,
destroying our stability,

and we were no longer just the land.

Birth

MARLIS MCCOLLUM

It was autumn when you twisted down
in Mother's belly, pressed head
to bony gate and swirled
into expectant hands,

autumn when wind plucked leaves from twig
at stem and rocked them feather-light to ground,
to gather like bright plumage from some great bird
shaken into life.

Papa's Pockets

YOLONDA NICELY

I am from the cold of a long winter night
when your pockets were empty

I am from the need to forget hunger pains
when your pockets were empty

I am from your wants that could not be fulfilled
when your pockets were empty

I am from the sadness of your eyes
when your pockets were empty

I am from the stretch of your hands to hold
on to life when your pockets were empty

If your pockets were full, I would not be

Waste Not, Want Not

MAXINE COMPOSTO

Yikes! I've just dumped half a bottle of cinnamon into my morning mocha java. Now what? Shall I throw it away? No, of course not. That's wasteful. "Waste not, want not" is woven into my DNA.

I've always had plenty of everything. But my parents? They did not. They grew up during the Great Depression and World War II. My dad once ate soap because he was so hungry. It looked like a slice of potato. Dad thought that being drafted into the Army during World War II was the best thing that had ever happened to him. He had more than enough clothing, three meals a day, and money in his pocket.

My mom pushed a plow behind a mule making furrows for planting. She picked cotton, corn, and beans. She milked cows and churned butter. She gathered eggs for breakfast and killed chickens for dinner. Mom received one pair of shoes every September, and by the end of the school year her toes pushed and heels jammed like rising dough overflowing its bowl. Clothes and shoes were passed among her seven brothers and sisters. When fabric was worn soft it was cut into squares and sewn together into quilts. Her mother always said, "waste not, want not," a lesson that Mom took to heart and passed on to me.

My parents had hard lives, but I did not. They were frugal so I could be a child. When I was growing up, my parents grew vegetables in our New York City backyard. I didn't take to gardening, canning, or cooking, but I yearned to be able to sew and knit. Mom kept our Singer sewing machine humming making my school clothes, party dresses, and play clothes. I watched her lay, pin, and cut fabric from Simplicity or McCall's patterns bought at the Five and Dime store. She also knitted and crocheted baby blankets, bonnets, and booties that seemed to spring from her needles. Eventually I learned to sew, knit, and crochet doll clothes. Painstakingly, Mom taught me her skills.

"I'll show you how to do this," she'd say after I made a mistake, and then she'd pull out what she had fixed. "Now you do it." I fumed, but I figured it out.

Dad laid brick after brick into soft cement to build our garage while I watched him and created mud pies and toad tunnels in a nearby sandbox. He also created a movable wall in our basement to separate it into two sections. A fishtank placed right in the middle provided a window into his workshop, where I could see his tools neatly organized on hooks hanging from a pocked piece of plywood. Little drawers contained different sizes of nails, screws, and washers. Dad would set me up with a hammer, nails, and a piece of wood to build a boat. I could see him, but I was far enough away from his tools—especially his electric saw—that I wouldn't get hurt. I yearned for him to teach me, but he was always too busy working. So I settled for just being near him.

It's been said that Dad saved the first dollar he ever made. He kept his 1949 green Plymouth for almost 10 years, repairing it until it could no longer climb hills. Even though he had enough money in his later years, he jury-rigged his old toaster oven with a paper clip to keep the door closed. He had a new toaster oven in a cabinet. When asked why he didn't just use the new one, he would reply, "waste not, want not."

This is why I'm staring at my morning mocha java with a half a bottle of cinnamon dumped into it. I can't throw it away. I decide to pour it into a smoothie. It tastes like sandy bark, but I choke it down.

Now my stomach begins sputtering and lurching. The cinnamon is searching for escape. I wonder if cinnamon could be toxic, so I Google it. Yes, too much cinnamon could damage my liver, give me cancer, or stop my breathing. Okay, Google. How much cinnamon is too much? According to WebMD, one-half to 1 teaspoon is the maximum a person should eat on any one day. Uh-oh. I'm beginning to sweat. My face feels like it's burning. I hyperventilate. I'm dizzy. I vomit.

I call my daughter and tell her what I did and where the will is.

"Mom, haven't you heard about the cinnamon challenges going on? It's all over TikTok."

"TikTok?"

"Some people have died from overdosing on cinnamon. Why didn't you just throw it away?" she moans.

"Waste not, want not," I say, as the sweat runs down my face.

Life on the Farm

MARY QUATTRO

There were six of us children growing up on a would-be farm in West Virginia. Daddy was a coal miner and worked long hours, so many of the daily chores were left to Mom and us kids.

We didn't raise crops, but we had animals that needed tending. We helped bring in the hay to feed the cows.

My younger brother drove the John Deere tractor—although he could barely reach the pedals—as we girls threw the hay bales on the slowly moving trailer headed to the barn.

We fed the thousands of chickens that came as peeps and left weeks later to become fryers on someone's table.

We fed the pigs—our least favorite job—and made our own games in the haylofts and in the groves of golden quaking aspen trees.

We chased fireflies at night, swam in the cool creek during the day, and had loud sibling fights and disruptions on a regular basis.

Our mother taught us to respect each other's property and to not be picky eaters.

We put milkweed sap on our poison ivy and played in the old cemetery just down the narrow lane from our farmhouse.

We went to a two-room schoolhouse by the river for first and second grades, walking along the railroad track to get there. My older sisters rode the bus to their high schools, and we younger ones did not envy them the trip.

We were privileged to live in our secluded refuge, although we didn't always appreciate it at the time—privileged to create our own games and build our own dreams.

Pastures
SUMMER HARDINGE

Trussed up straw bales lay stacked like bread loaves,
bundled as ready-made bricks in piles

and gravid dark mingled
with farming tools, sleds, buckets,

saddle soap. Two roughhewed slatted doors,
locks rusty and difficult to open,

 lent little light upon a mud-packed floor.
Stalls below and a hayloft above

with slats for windows, a pitchfork and grain
sacks, some pieces of lumber,

metal chest for bridles and a small red bicycle:
slowly objects formed.

All winter snow froze. The barn captured
our heat, and then steam rose,

made a greenhouse of vaulted timber, leather
and our breath.

       Tucked amongst steamed bales,

we thawed, imagined loosened
honeysuckle moving across summer fields. Things

scurried past sleep on rafters. Inside our strands of grain,
we built forty-pound bastions,

while hay dropped down
in soft thuds. Through the slats, sunlight lifted

us like fireflies.

The Kindness of Strangers

ROBIN SOFGE

Growing up in Akron, Ohio, my younger sister and I longed for the freedom to ride the public bus all by ourselves to Quaker Square, which was named after the oatmeal company whose grain silos and mill had been transformed into an upscale shopping area.

When we were about 6 and 7 years old, Mom said Becky and I could go alone, but only if we had memorized our address and phone number. Once we passed Mom's test, we were eager for our trip of a lifetime. We had studied the bus route map well in advance and waited at the bus stop long before the bus arrived. Finally, after what seemed like an eternity, the big silver bus screeched to a halt and opened its heavy doors.

Becky and I raced up the giant steps and deposited our coins for bus fare in the box, listening to them plunk to the bottom.

"Where are you girls headed?" the bus driver asked.

"Quaker Square!" we said at the same time, collapsing into giggles.

Smiling, the driver instructed us to tug on the plastic cord above our seats before our stop, which would alert him that we wanted to get off. The bus ride went without a hitch.

After an afternoon of window shopping for items that were well above our weekly allowance, we ended the day by ordering decadent banana splits from Barnhill's Ice Cream Parlor.

The banana splits appeared on the counter before us piled high with whipped cream, chocolate jimmies, and bright red maraschino cherries. But after the teenage cashier rang up the order, I realized I hadn't counted my money right.

"Oh no," I said, my hands starting to shake as I peered into my wallet.

"What?" Becky asked.

"I don't have enough money." My face turned red and I started to sweat. "Do you have any money I can borrow?"

"I just have an extra quarter. I need the rest for bus fare home," Becky said, showing me the contents of her own sparse wallet.

I sheepishly looked at the cashier, who was well aware there was some drama unfolding.

"Can we cancel the order? We don't have enough money for this and our bus fare home, too."

"Don't worry about it," said the cashier. "You just enjoy them. Keep your money. They're on the house."

I was so embarrassed. "Thanks," I said. "We're not going to eat the banana splits though."

"Why not?" the cashier asked. "I can't resell strawberry, pistachio, and rocky road ice cream banana splits, you know. I'm just going to throw them out if you don't eat them. Really. It's not a problem. It was an honest mistake."

Becky and I picked up a big stack of napkins and brought the glorious mountains of ice cream covered with gooey syrups to the table. We felt such relief and joy as we gobbled up our scrumptious treats.

I'll always remember the thrill of that first bus ride adventure with my sister and the kindness of the cashier, who didn't shame me for not having enough money to pay. Ice cream has never tasted so sweet.

Art Lesson

JOANNE LOZAR GLENN

They saved it for Fridays. Every teacher had the same projects. Fall: iron leaves between waxed paper. Winter: chalk snow scenes on black construction paper. Spring: draw daffodils.

Except for Miss Malik. She was young, pretty, and not a nun.

"Bring lots of newspapers and a light bulb for Art this week," she told us one day. So that night, after changing my uniform and before memorizing my Baltimore catechism, I made sure to tuck the supplies into my schoolbag. I liked Miss Malik. She'd put together a class poetry book and included my poem.

First Friday: We spread oilcloth on desktops to keep them clean, then layered each light bulb with strip after strip of hand-dipped newspaper soaked in wheat paste. Its slimy crust thickened our fingers till they could hardly move.

Second Friday: We painted the bulbs with tempera and set them on the windowsill to dry.

Third and final Friday: The big day. We were to smash the bulb against our desks until we heard the glass break.

"This is a maraca," Miss Malik told us. "In Mexico, it's used to make music."

It was the '60s, and all we knew of Mexico was bandits wearing big sombreros in black-and-white TV Westerns. Miss Malik's lesson let us glimpse another world. And she'd taught us that something broken—even when it was broken on purpose, deeply, where no one could see—could still sing.

Where I'm From

MARY AXIOTIS

after George Ella Lyon

I'm from a country far away,
Where gods ruled the world.

I'm from a country of sunshine and sandy beaches,
Old cities and ancient ruins.

I'm from a country that suffered under empires,
But survived and flourished.

I'm from a country that built civilizations
And brought me here.

I'm from immigrants who walked
Thousands of miles to safety.

I'm from the hands of my grandparents
And the heart of my parents who raised me.

I'm from old pictures and wrinkled faces
That wore sorrow and suffering.

I'm from a culture of worshippers
Who believed in freedom and brought me here.

I'm from here now
And for the rest of my life.

Herstory

Elegy

MAGGIE BUTLER

I.

Daughters swim on this sultry evening;
the contented laugh of summer's children
lingers in the humid air.
The grass, Kentucky Blue, is trim
but not fussy, and flattened in places
from afternoon play.

The vegetable garden is rich,
extravagant actually, and each morning
after the crickets go to sleep and when
the birds are waking, I wade through
squash and beans,
tomatoes and peas,
strawberries and basil,
prowling for all that is ripe and ready for us.

For no apparent reason the tea garden
sighs a whirl of spearmint and peppermint,
blending notes of lemon and orange mints, too,
and when I look to see what caused the stir,
I pause instead to watch the heavy sun
make its graceful slip into the white pines that separate
us from the forest, and where the Great Horned Owl
comes to visit us now and again.

You're standing by the pool, large as life,
tossing slippery fish-girls back
into the water over and over,

and it's how you look in moments like this
that continue to find restless sleep in my heart.

II.

I keep your picture in my drawer and sometimes
I take it out and try to imagine

how you would look . . . how you would feel

if you were here now, and not still standing in
Branson's field, forever thirty and leaning
against a vibrant maple tree, its lowest branch
resting on the sleeve of your favourite shirt,
faded from too many washings and with
the L-shaped tear on the pocket
I always intended to mend.

2,000 Albums

CINDY ATLEE

When we were married, there were times when I hated that record collection. 2,000 albums collected over many years: first when he was in the Navy, then as a professional deejay, and finally as part of an avid avocation. 2,000 albums that had to be packed, boxed, lifted, moved, uncrated, sorted, and reshelved every time we moved. 2,000 albums that seemed to take up every nook and cranny of every living room we ever had.

2,000 albums, including the latest recording from the artist whose concert we'd seen on our very first date. He'd shown up that night in a Jeep borrowed from a friend. In an open-air Jeep on an unseasonably cold October night. In an open-air Jeep so noisy we had to shout at each other as we drove to the concert. In an open-air Jeep just unsafe enough to make me wonder if seeing Bob was worth it—because at the beginning of that night I was far more interested in Dylan than in the man behind the wheel of that Jeep, although by the end of it those positions had been reversed.

2,000 albums that our toddler daughter delighted in pulling down from the shelves, teething on them almost, as her father sprang up to prevent an atrocity from being committed on the seminal work of Frank Zappa or the earliest rebellious edges of Neil Young or even the guilty pleasure of the Monkees singing "I'm a Believer." Oh, he was such a believer in the music, in those 2,000 albums, in the power of music to stir the soul.

2,000 albums that included some of the last music John Lennon would ever record, music he played as he wept when the news came in, during his overnight FM radio shift, that John had been shot and killed.

2,000 albums that included everything U2 had ever recorded, starting with a bootleg LP he'd bought after seeing them in the tiny Ontario Theatre in Washington, D.C., playing to what seemed like only a handful of attendees who believed as he did that they were on to something great.

2,000 measures of a man's life, meted out through the ebullience of Bob Seger, the doomed beauty of Eva Cassidy, the folksy wisdom of John Prine, the husky sensuality of Chrissie Hynde.

2,000 albums that help form the common ground between his son and his daughter, born 20 years apart, raised by different women, each still answering the Grateful Dead's call to jam—their hearts beating with music, as his did.

2,000 albums I moved for the last time, without him, 15 years ago.

His remains.

A Life in Couches

SHAYNE JOHNSON

The first couch my husband and I purchased as newlyweds was from a now-defunct store called Persnickety in the Pentagon City Mall. It was a gorgeous double-cushioned floral sofa in soft greens and yellows. I don't know why, but I fell in love with this couch immediately and had to have it. I was feeling flush with cash after some generous wedding checks, and this felt like an important step in our married life. I kept my eye on this couch for quite a while before bringing my husband to the store to visit. At this point, our living room furniture consisted of one green upholstered chair, courtesy of his grandparents. To this day, my husband and I both remember my tears as I argued that spending over $1,000 on a couch (this was 30 years ago) was perfectly reasonable. He may not have agreed with me, but he did agree to the couch. Looking back, I see that flower fabric as indicative of our new life together. We were in the spring of our marriage and our couch reflected this. We had that couch for close to 10 years, through two homes and one baby. I loved it, but eventually my tastes changed, the cushions began to sag, and our little dog made a permanent dent on one side. It no longer fit the style of our home.

This may be because our home also changed. In our life together, my husband and I have purchased more homes than couches, and sometimes it is a big change that necessitates the smaller one. Our next couch was a classic from Pottery Barn: three cushions this time, and cherry red. Since we've had so little red in our homes over the years, I still can't believe we went for it. I do know that we had learned by then that white upholstery is always a bad idea. Maybe the darker color was more practical now that we had a baby and a toddler. Another selling point for the Pottery Barn couch was the removable and washable slipcovers. After the couch was in place, we spent a year tussling over which rug to buy. Finally, we compromised on a cherry red and purple geometric rug that matched perfectly.

This seems indicative of a more mature marriage—learning each other's style and taste, compromising.

This couch also moved with us, this time across the country to California. But as our family grew, so did my longing for a sectional. Our cherry couch was fine, but we now had three children, and we all wanted to sit together on the couch. This couch, in our cozy family room next to an open-plan kitchen, still had only the vintage recliner to keep it company. Whoever had to sit in the recliner felt like they were being put in a time-out, including my husband.

Still, it wasn't until we decided to do some larger scale remodeling that this couch was shown an exit. Finally we had a new custom sectional couch where we could all curl up together and watch TV. But there was trouble in paradise: our neighbors' dogs barked incessantly, and my husband became cranky and anxious from the noise. (There is more to the story, but that's for a different essay.) We moved the almost-new, soft and deep purple sectional into our new home just a few miles away. Here we were able to enjoy it for another nine years. Did I think this would be our forever home or our forever couch? Not really, but our time on the purple couch was great. Our family grew up, we watched TV shows and movies, opened gifts on Christmas morning, and spent sick days on this couch.

While the purple sectional served as the heart of our living room, another made its way into our home. Our house had an older layout, and we knocked down a wall to create a family room off the kitchen. Here is where our current couch enters: a midcentury modern sunflower yellow leather couch that we are still enjoying. Bought from a local store in our city, this couch has served us well. When we moved from California back to Virginia four years ago, this is the couch that came with us. There was only room for one, and our purple sectional had run its course. I was tired of the color by then and ready to part with it. So now the golden yellow couch sits proudly in my living room. It's not our TV couch, but our cozy couch. We use it the most during the colder months—sitting by the fire, reading, talking. We celebrate Christmas on this couch and our dogs regularly nap on it. Our kids have grown up and are in college or in their own apartments. It's not getting the wear and tear of our previous couches, and we have no plans to move. This one may take the record for our longest lasting couch. It does hold the record for the most homes: it has lived in three to date.

As I write this, I think of all the other items that we choose to surround ourselves with that mark our lives: dining room tables, bed covers, paint colors, and even coffee makers. I think of art I have bought while traveling or been given by those I love, of books that have stood the test of time and moves. Each Christmas, the unwrapping of ornaments provides another way to view my life—the people who have surrounded me, the places we have gone, the things that matter. Some things stay with us and decorate our lives for a season and some for a lifetime. We have weathered a lot of changes, homes, moves, and jobs in 30 years. I am happy to report that while I like replacing my couches about every 10 years, I have never wanted to replace my husband, and vice versa.

Reading Glasses

MARION SHEAFFER

I reach for mine
and you grab yours.
Little reading glasses
help us see the newspaper
as we drink our coffee
in contented silence.

I push mine down
the bridge of my nose
to look at you
the very moment
you peer over yours
to look at me.

A smile flickers
across your face
before you return
to the news of the day.
No need to say
anything.

Reading glasses,
like hourglasses,
mark the passage
of time. We are
growing old
together.

Peace Like a River

LYNN HAYS

As a lifelong Catholic, it wasn't until my husband and I began attending a Presbyterian church that I learned to love traditional hymns. Familiar musical scores and beautifully written lyrics, led by a choir who encouraged everyone to join in, equaled faith made manifest. Bob had grown up singing in the choir, and now we harmonized, shoulder to shoulder. Often I found myself humming a hymn during the week. One Sunday I was delighted to learn that the Psalms were sung by the Hebrews as they walked. Prayer in motion.

One of my favorite hymns is Horatio Spafford's "It Is Well With My Soul." He wrote it while trying to cope with the deep pain of losing his four daughters in a shipwreck.

> When peace, like a river, attendeth my way,
> When sorrows, like sea billows roll;
> Whatever my lot, Thou hast taught me to say,
> It is well, it is well with my soul.

After my husband's sudden death from cardiac arrest, I remained calm and introspective in my grieving. I've read that this is a common trauma response, but all I knew at the time was that I felt numb and empty. What soothed me was mentally mouthing this hymn. Contemplating life's big questions and my own mortality, it lessened my constant fears.

That calm was tested five years later on December 21, 2016.

My daughter Brooks and I were on a short vacation in Cartagena, Colombia. After walking the city in 90-degree heat, we decided to take a boat ride to the Rosario Islands. We boarded one of the smaller boats tied up at the busy port. Like a small airplane, the boat had sets of two seats on either side of a center aisle, seating a total of 36. It looked a little low in the water, but it had a bimini top for shade and two engines to power across 15 miles of the Caribbean. We were promised a 45-minute ride to the little island, where staff would serve lunch on the beach before we returned. There were sunny skies and a quick breeze. The sound of happy chatter in multiple languages surrounded us as we found our seats. We were on the port (left) side of the boat, with Brooks by the water and me in the aisle; two others sat across the aisle on my right.

The captain steered us slowly toward open waters. Although it had been calm in the protected port, the wind and waves picked up in open water. We swayed a bit for the first 20 minutes, but the warm sun and good cheer among the passengers kept us calm. I was fascinated by the man sitting in front of me who wore a banana-yellow one-piece tankini with an iPhone and water bottle fastened to the belt around his waist. I'm pretty certain I was staring as he pulled out his phone and began to take selfies.

Suddenly a strong wave hit us from the side, startling everyone on board, and the wind became more intense. The captain was trying to steer the bow into the wind, but one of the engines was faltering and he was having difficulty controlling it. People were still smiling but squealing as the boat started to toss in earnest. The waves were about four to five feet high by now, which put them almost even with the deck. Brooks looked at my alarmed face and said, "*Tranquilidad*, Mama. They do this every day." As the daughter of a career Coast Guard Captain, I replied that I was sure they didn't do this with whitecaps, but just then, as the bow of the boat rose to try to cut through a wave, the engines cut out and the bow went down instead. Water rushed into the boat until the front was underwater. Then we were slammed by a large wave on the left, pulling our side underwater and flipping the boat upside down.

Underwater. I kept my eyes closed against the stinging seawater and held my breath as I felt kicking feet on my head and shoulders. I knew the people on the right side of the boat must have fallen on top of us, pinning us underwater. There was silent motion all around me. *Don't breathe. Don't breathe.* I was calm, not panicked. *Don't breathe. Just wait. Don't breathe.* "*When peace like a river...*" I felt peaceful, calm, sluggish even. I didn't want to fight to get to the surface; I wanted to relax in this quiet space. I heard a siren call in the water. It whispered, "See what staying will bring. What questions will be answered." I had thought so many times about dying after I was widowed. My soul was in order, and I had reconciled myself to life's brevity. *Don't breathe. Don't breathe.* Then nothing. *Breathe.* Nothing.

Nothing because I was above water. The boat was completely underwater, disappeared. I took a big gulp of air and opened my eyes, squinting in the light. My glasses and hat were lost, so I looked for Brooks through slitted eyes. There were people scattered everywhere, frantically calling for their family members. Brooks shouted, "Swim to me, over here, away from where the boat was." I swam to her voice, awkwardly, because by some miracle my sandals had stayed on my feet. Others were swimming in all directions, and I could hazily see small pleasure boats in the nearby channel. Some of these were steering toward the swimmers.

I reached Brooks, who had caught the attention of an approaching boat. We kept swimming as the boat slowly motored towards us. Soon they were helping me, Brooks, and two others onboard, including the man in the yellow tankini. Other boats began to arrive, picking up two, three, four, or however many extras their boats would hold. The boat that picked us up had been chartered by a lovely woman who was scattering the ashes of her dead sister. I asked the name of her sister and said a prayer of gratitude for our rescue.

Our small boat was the second to make it to the island. Soon other boats started to arrive, and people were accounting for everyone in their party. The Colombian Coast Guard showed up and counted people, writing down their names. People sobbed and hugged as they located friends and family—all except for one woman and her father, whose mother/ wife was still unaccounted for even as the last of the small boats docked.

There were towels and a restroom on this tiny island, along with a kitchen where the staff was preparing lunch. Wet, frightened people sat in the sun trying to dry out and calm down. I was already calm, numb, with a throbbing head. As Brooks talked to the man in the tankini, I went to find the restroom. *"It is well, it is well with my soul."* Once there, I bent over to examine a gash on my ankle and was surprised when water poured out of my nose—not a trickle, but a river, flowing freely. *"When peace, like a river…"* It was a faucet turned on full force, burning, and I could taste salt in my throat. I looked at the large puddle on the bathroom floor, pooled around my feet. I tried but couldn't remember. Had I inhaled water? Brooks told me that she remembered swimming between the bimini top and the side of the boat to get free and come to the surface. I couldn't remember doing that. I only remembered being underwater and then nothing until finding myself above water, gulping air. How was so much in my head instead of in my lungs?

So many questions.

I rejoined the group, and the staff brought out lunch. The Colombian Coast Guard kept nervously checking their list, hoping the lost woman had simply been overlooked. Hours passed, and when we asked if we would get back while it was still light, the Coast Guard said they weren't sure. They didn't have a boat large enough for all 35. We might have to spend the night on the beach. That's when Brooks and the man in the tankini used his iPhone 7 (the first iPhone to be waterproof) to call the American embassy. The people on the boat were from many countries, but with a group of U.S. citizens on board, our embassy said they would send a boat for us all.

After a less frightening return boat ride, our bedraggled crew was greeted by reporters and police when we disembarked. We were asked by the embassy rescuers not to speak with anyone, and we were taken by bus to various points of the city to walk back to our hotels. Most were barefoot. I was one of the lucky few to have sandals for the walk.

Postscript: Two days later, the body of the missing woman was found with the sunken boat. Her clothes had caught in her seat.

The Decision

TINA MCCOY

My husband George and I had been married seven years when I began to suspect something was not right. He often traveled to Asia for business, but this time his normal daily phone calls had become less frequent, and when I called him at night he didn't answer the phone.

Once when I called, he answered the phone but said he couldn't talk. When I asked if he had someone with him in the room, he said yes; when I asked if that person was male or female, he didn't respond. George had always been honest with me, telling me everything he did, but this time was different. He seemed distant.

On his last trip he called me once a week, just to find out how I was doing. When I told him that I missed him and felt lonely at night, he told me not to worry, that he was coming home in two weeks. Finally he called to tell me he was flying back home to Dallas in two days and would arrive at night. This news lifted my spirits. In preparation for his arrival, I cleaned the house, bought fresh flowers for the living room, and baked his favorite pecan pie.

The night George was to arrive, I waited up all night, but he didn't come home. I worried that something had happened to him or the aircraft. *Where was he? Why didn't he call me?* His colleagues said George had been at the airport with them but had caught another flight; his friends in Dallas hadn't heard from him. Finally, I called the airline to inquire if George had been on the flight to Dallas, and they told me his name was not on the boarding list. Feeling helpless, I cried in frustration. There was nothing I could do except wait until he called.

On the third day, I was standing in the kitchen in front of the refrigerator when the phone rang. It was George. In a normal voice, he told me he was in Houston for work and had visited his friend Glenn in Baytown, Texas. He continued in a nonchalant tone, "I'm sorry, but I couldn't come home because I brought someone from Asia with me." I was silent. I felt a lump in my throat and my heart pounded as he continued, "I still love you, but I want to marry Nani. That's why I brought her and her son here." In shock, I hung up the phone, ran to the bedroom, and cried all day.

I felt betrayed, ashamed, and full of self-doubt. *Was I not good enough for him? Did I do something wrong to cause him to leave me for another woman?* My heart ached, and I threw up. I felt like my body was torn apart, and my head hurt like someone had beaten me. I felt stupid for not seeing this coming.

The next morning, I drove to Baytown to confront the woman in Glenn's front yard.

"Why did you come here?" I demanded.

"George brought me," she said.

"Did you not know that he's married?"

She lowered her gaze. "Yes."

"So why did you come here with him anyway?" I asked in a sharp tone. I was so angry I felt like hitting her.

In a hushed voice she replied, "He said you wouldn't mind."

Now I was getting angrier, not toward her, but toward George. At the same time, I felt myself falling apart and slipping into the abyss. I wanted to cry but held my tears, too proud to cry in front of her. I wanted to know the truth, and asked again why George brought her to the U.S.

Looking directly into my eyes, she replied, "He said you are separated from him."

"He lied to you," I said. "We are not separated. We are married and we live happily together in Dallas. We loved each other...." My words trailed off. I noticed that I said "loved." I wondered, *Why did I say that in the past tense? Is that true?*

She looked at me, confused. "Do you love him?" she asked.

Feeling slightly embarrassed, I mumbled, "Of course. That's why we've been married for seven years, and I'm not going to let him go."

"He wants to marry me," she said, then slowly, carefully, added, "because you don't care for him."

I froze and stared at her. She looked so naive, I felt pity for her. I held her gaze, and for a split second a thought crossed my mind, *Yes, I don't care for him anymore*. I felt it deep inside me. Suddenly my anger blazed, and I wanted to divorce him right away. But I needed to know one more thing: "Do you love him?"

She looked embarrassed, but responded in a soft voice, "Maybe, I don't know. He is good to my son." At that moment she looked vulnerable and ashamed, and I felt for her. I know that in Asia, divorced women don't get second chances. They are branded as used goods, and no one wants to touch or marry them, especially if they have children. I didn't know what to say. She had come so far from Malaysia to make a home and create a family for her son, albeit at my expense. I was fortunate that I didn't have any children, and had more opportunities here in the U.S.

With tears in my eyes, I left her in the front yard and drove back to Dallas. I was emotionally exhausted. But that night I fell asleep with my mind made up. I decided to walk away from my marriage and let George marry that woman.

The Drunken Ladies of the Garden Club

DIANA READ

It was ironic, thought Sophie Martin, that the eve of her first anniversary—the anniversary of her first year without alcohol—should coincide with the hazard of a possible slip from abstinence. Usually, garden club meetings occurred on Saturday mornings and the refreshments were coffee and cake.

However, this Sunday brunch at the end of April was also the annual fundraiser, and there would be champagne. Had it been just champagne, Sophie would not have worried, but this champagne would be mixed with orange juice, and she was afraid—very afraid—that she would accidentally sip a mimosa without realizing it contained more than orange juice. In her mind's ear she could hear one of the axioms of AA: "A sip can lead to a slip."

"Sophie!" She turned to see Irene, her hostess, hailing her. "Welcome! Are you ready for the competition today?" Under the guidance of a senior member, the others would create a bouquet. The winner would receive a gift certificate from Merrivale Nurseries.

"Yes, thanks, Irene. Thanks for hostessing the brunch! Everything looks lovely." Not only did the terrace, set up with umbrella-shaded tables, look festive, but the floppy straw hats and flowered dresses of the ladies created a light-hearted ambiance.

Mimi grabbed her arm. "Sophie! Come sit by me!" Sophie followed her to a table. "Look!" Mimi said. "There's a mimosa right by your plate."

Oh, no! What was she going to do? "Ah…you know, darling, there's no telling who might have already sipped from this glass. I'll get a fresh one."

Sophie went to the long table covered with a white cloth, champagne flutes, bottles of champagne reposing in ice buckets, and pitchers of orange juice. The bartender was a tall woman dressed in a white uniform jacket and a toque that covered her hair. An ordinary woman, Sophie would have thought, except for a faint shimmer in the air around her, as though she were giving off heat waves.

"Do you have a fake mimosa?" Sophie asked. "You know, sparkling water and orange juice, no alcohol?"

The bartender's intelligent gray eyes looked into hers. "Of course. One moment."

She knows, Sophie thought.

The bartender took a bottle of sparkling water from under the table, poured it into a flute, added orange juice. "Here you are."

"Thank you." Sophie gave her a grateful smile.

Five minutes later Irene looked a little flustered. "Ladies, I'm afraid the caterers are delayed, so please just chat among yourselves until they arrive."

"Good," Mimi said. "More mimosas!"

The bartender moved among the four tables, pouring drinks for the ladies. By the time the caterers arrived with the scrambled eggs, warm croissants, apricot pastries, and strawberry tarts, most of them were quite far gone.

"Over here," Mimi called to her, holding up her flute for a refill. "We need more at this table, pleash!" She grabbed a couple of flutes off the tray, setting one down in front of Sophie.

"Oh, no, have this one, it's fresher," the bartender said. "I made it especially for you." She smiled at Sophie, who immediately felt relieved.

After the plates were cleared away and the tables brushed down, Felicity Payne-Townsend, her British accent still evident despite 30 years' residence in Virginia, stood up. "Ladies, today I'm going to show you how to make May baskets," she said. "May baskets were a charming custom that has now been subsumed by the Easter tradition of baskets full of sweets for children. However, a century ago people would rise before dawn to hang May baskets on their neighbors' front doorknobs. The baskets were filled with flowers in the May colors of green, blue, and white."

"Thash nice," Mimi said.

Felicity distributed squares of thick white paper and rolls of cellotape.

"I'll show you how to roll these squares into cones," she said.

"Why a cone? Why not a basket?" Gillian asked.

"Most people already have too much stuff," Felicity said. "With a paper cone, you can throw the whole thing away after the flowers die." She proceeded to create a May basket with blue satin ribbons, green ferns, and blue and white flowers spilling over the sides. "Now, how are you all doing?"

She walked around to inspect the ladies' efforts. All except Sophie were so drunk, or at least tipsy, that their attempts at rolling the paper into cones and taping them were a failure. Some couldn't even punch holes at the top of the cones to thread the ribbon through. Those who did thread the ribbon mashed the ferns and blue flowers flat. Sophie was the only member to create a May bouquet that looked like Felicity's.

"I guessh I had too many mimoshahs," Mimi confided. "I jush love them."

"The prize goes to Sophie," Felicity announced. "Congratulations!"

Sophie heaved a sigh of relief. The bronze chip she would receive tomorrow to mark her one-year anniversary was safe. That was the real win, although the gift certificate would be very welcome. She rose to collect the envelope from Felicity, thanked her, then walked to the bar.

"Thank you…" she leaned forward to read the name tag on the bartender's jacket, "…Flora. Oh, like the Goddess Flora!"

The bartender smiled. "Exactly like the Goddess Flora," she said.

Sophie turned and began to walk away, but something made her turn around for one last glance. The bartender was no longer visible, but on the bar itself lay a garland of flowers.

Pedal Power

LAURA STURZA

My excitement about getting a brand new 12-speed bike was dampened when my scientist father conducted his usual months of research. He pored over *Consumer Reports* to be sure he'd pick the perfect item for his daughter's upcoming 16th birthday. My only other bike had been a one-speed we got from a yard sale. I had longed for a fancy replacement for years. Little did Dad know, I was also dreaming about how his planned gift would give me autonomy. I'd have a getaway vehicle.

Dad drove me 45 minutes into D.C. to Big Wheel Bikes, which he chose because he had learned the store was highly rated. Outside, I stood looking up at the shop's enormous painted sign of a bike silhouette on a yellow background. Although my father's investigative style nearly sucked the joy out of any purchase, when I saw the model he'd pre-selected— touched it, smelled the rubber of the tires—I fell into a trance. It was silver (my favorite metal), a unisex bike then called a mixte.

All these years later, I remember the salesman's name: Barry. He adjusted the seat height and handlebars, then sent me for a test ride. It was lightweight, a racing bike, something to fly on. I returned to the store breathless, grinning. I didn't often feel that kind of happiness with Dad. I was never sure when he might swat it down. But that morning, I thought I saw a slight smile on his face as he paid the bill.

My best friend Jenny was a year older, and so cool she tooled around on a moped. She asked me if I had named my new wheels. I hadn't. But considering that Graham Nash was one of my music crushes and nothing was more romantic than the idea of dating one of Joni Mitchell's exes, I dubbed the bike Nash. It made sense since my fantasy exit strategy from my parents' house usually involved a man who'd take me away.

In high school, Nash offered respite from our chaotic home. When Dad and I had a dust-up, I was out of there. I became a hardcore biker, often racking up 20 miles.

After college, I transferred my musical affection to David Bowie, but still schlepped Nash to my new homes. The gears didn't turn for a few years, though. I had moved on to yoga, dancing, and hikes with a Walkman strapped to my waist.

Dad and I got along better when I was an adult. When I moved across country in my mid-30s, it wasn't to get away from an angry parent. I was moving toward an adventure—the Southwest, with its cacti set against tie-dyed violet and orange sunsets. While downsizing for my cross-country move, I let that lovely bicycle go. Other elements of my teenage self came along—my creative bent, rebelliousness, and intense physicality. Plus my doubts that I was lovable and my sensitivity.

It would be years before another bike got my attention. As it's turned out, there have been only two of them in my life. As a serial monogamist, I give my heart away slowly.

For my 55th birthday, Mom gave me a check, with her familiar cursive signature on it. "Pick out something you'd like," she said.

While cycling hadn't been in my life for decades, I drove straight to a shop near my new home in Los Angeles. The salesperson, Isabelle, was a charming 19-year-old punk rocker, adorned in tats. I imagined she had a complicated relationship with her parents, like I did at her age.

Along with her edginess, she was kind. When I told her I hadn't been a biker since my late teens, she said, "I love getting people back on bikes."

My Dad had died years earlier. I'd done none of his hyper-research, a style I'd co-opted from him. Instead, I let Isabelle guide me to one that was muscular and platinum colored.

The smile on my face when I took it for a test ride was as big as the one after my first spin on Nash. Except my adventures were no longer reliant on a fantasy man who'd swoop me off to Santa Fe and L.A., dreamy places I'd discovered on my own.

Isabelle made the sale. I didn't tell her I'd decided to name my new bike Izzy.

My legs are as sturdy as when I was I sixteen. When I stand on them, they are more solidly fixed to the ground than my younger legs were. On rides through Griffith Park, trees blur, sunlight warms me, wind slices through my ancient Joni Mitchell t-shirt.

I am no longer conjuring up escape routes. Izzy is my smack-talking sidekick. I am the one driving her.

Shifting Out of Neutral

CHRISTINE KOUBEK

I'm usually too fixated on my laptop's screen to notice my compatriots at Starbucks, but two girls dressed in the *joie-de-vivre* colors of girlhood made me pause—one in a flamingo-pink shirt, the other in electric blue pants and sneakers as green as fresh grass. Listening to them, I couldn't help but remember what it was like to be 13 or 14, remember—as I sat there in blue jeans and black—what it was like before the color leaked out.

As the girls whispered, my mind's photo album flipped back to myself pre-college, pre-work, pre-marriage, and pre-motherhood, to a time when I wandered the mall with Ferris Bueller's mentality that leisure rules. I'd browse through stores and inhale the crisp scent of new clothes I couldn't afford, or visit a beloved purple jacket I'd put on layaway. It was a time of longing for something about to be.

Now I was in the middle of the middle years, and so many big milestones had passed: choosing a career, getting married, buying a house, having children. I had long ago turned my focus to my sons' interests and dreams, content to fill my days with their school performances, sports games, and our extended family's events. And though I could now afford more things, time spent coordinating clothes wasn't one of them. I'd come to love the simplicity of black.

Glancing out the window past the girls, I tried to recall the last time I wore red, the color my mother always said looked best on me. I had a favorite pair of red Reeboks in college, a red suit jacket during my first years of work in Boston, and a ruby dress that I wore to a holiday office party. The dress resulted in a date with a cute guy.

But I slowly stopped wearing that cardinal color, or anything bold for that matter, unless I was in the Caribbean, or suddenly 10 pounds lighter, or in just the right mood. That was the real difference: mood. Recent years had offered so many opportunities to grapple with gray, from the challenges of childrearing to deaths that hit closer and closer to home.

Looking back, I could spot signs of fading. That girl in red had toned down to a late twenty-something who wore an occasional colorful shirt or scarf, and then was further muted during the early years of motherhood, when efficiency ruled: black, white, gray, beige, and always a little black dress. A convenient wardrobe that had morphed into a habit.

As I drove to my younger son's basketball game that afternoon, I remembered something my mother had said a few weeks earlier, when I was on my way to visit her in upstate New York. "I'm wearing brighter colors lately," she announced. "You won't believe it's me."

"What kind of colors?" My mother was in her 60s and had worn dark colors for as long as I could remember.

"You just wait until you see my closet," she said proudly.

Sure enough, it was full of vibrant hues. "Are you going on a trip? Has something happened? What have you done with my mother?"

She laughed. "No—I just thought it would be fun to add some spice."

After decades of working and raising my siblings and me alone, I figured this was my mother's way of finding a new side of herself. She had been out hiking and on road trips recently, too, things I had never seen her do.

The night after I got home from visiting my mother, I stood in my closet staring at rods full of neutral clothes and wondered what happened to the tomboy teenager I once was, the girl who got thrown from a horse and a Yamaha dirt bike, the latter my own fault.

I had begged my high school boyfriend for weeks to try his bike. I wanted to feel its weight in my hands, feel what it was like to have the wind not on my cheek as I peeked out from behind him, but across my face. It was our second time out. He was on his brother's bike, and I on his. "Let's go a little faster," he yelled over the engine noise. "Remember, when you shift from first to second, make sure your foot doesn't slip it to neutral."

Only that's exactly what I did, right as I gave it gas. The bike flipped. I flew into a tall patch of grass, the wind knocked out of me, but unhurt.

Seconds later he was crouched beside me, his helmet off. He looked frustrated, but didn't reprimand or say I told you so, only thank God the bike hadn't landed on me.

"I'll walk the bike back to your truck," I said.

"Walk back?" he smiled. "You can't just quit because you got stuck in neutral."

And here I was, more than 20 years later, in a closet dominated by neutral and with a dawning realization that I'd spent most of my 30s telling myself why I shouldn't do something instead of thinking about how I could.

That week, I spent an hour at the mall and came home with a cabernet-colored blouse, purple running shorts, and an emerald-green cardigan—not to be worn all at once. The day I wore the cardigan a friend said, "You look great!" while we waited at the bus stop. It was a day I said yes to an assignment I'd worried might be over my head. That evening, my husband said, "I love that green on you." I wondered what I must have looked like before. Is it the color or how you feel when you wear it?

A couple months later, I pondered that question again when a priest in an amethyst robe delivered an interesting take on Christmas. Instead of telling the story of Jesus' birth, he gave a simple sermon about how all birthdays are a celebration of the number of years someone has been a light on this planet. I sat on that hard wooden pew and thought about that, thought about the grayness of getting older, and wondered if it had to be that way. If our light, like our health, naturally diminishes as we get older, or if we can continue to keep it illuminated through our choices.

Fast forward four years. Much more than my closet has changed. I went to graduate school for a Master of Fine Arts degree, spent a week with my family in Peru distributing shoes to those in need during our first service trip, and went out dancing with friends again. In the process, I discovered that paying more attention to the colors I wear (even when I choose black) reminds me to think about what's possible.

Green is my new favorite. I wore it for my first half-marathon, which I ran in part for the challenge, and to show myself, as well as my sons, that if you're fortunate enough to grow older, life gives you many seasons to bloom.

Metamorphosis

SUSAN IVES MCCOLLUM

Like most women I know, I have struggled with body image through-out my life. I first became aware of mine around age 8, when I looked in the mirror and saw a chubby girl with scads of freckles staring back at me. Where my friends might have had a light sprinkling of freckles, mine rambled across the bridge of my nose, across my cheeks and forehead, and up and down my arms and legs like marching ants. My mom called my freckles "angel kisses." She shared stories of how she used to scrub her face to get her freckles off, or bleach them with lemon juice. She admitted none of her home remedies made any difference. I decided not to follow her lead and accepted my freckles as a sign of wholesomeness—the girl-next-door look.

When my torso started to thicken around age 10, I felt ashamed of my body. A picture from that time shows me in a one-piece bathing suit and rubber swim cap, my head dipped as I look shyly into the camera. I do not look happy to be photographed with my plump tummy and slight hint of a waistline. My bathing suit has a feminine touch. White and pink striped ruffles wrap across the bodice, giving one the sense of budding womanhood. Ruffles around the hips, dipping into a V in front, are meant to fool the eye into thinking the swimmer is slim. My hair is snugly tucked inside a white rubber bathing cap that sports a strap under the chin. It's a 1950s look that the Olympic ballet swimmers wore. Their caps had a rubber flower on the side to make them look fashionable. Mine, though, is plain and unadorned, just as I am—a fish out of water.

At 10, my body was just beginning to whisper of how it would mature. Two years later, I shot up to my current 5'7" and lost my chunky frame. I developed curves and breasts. My stomach flattened and my hips began to widen. I felt like a stranger in this new body. I suffered from painful cramps whenever I had a period, and experienced strange tingly feelings when I saw a cute boy. I started to care about my hair. It was auburn, thick, coarse, and unmanageable. My home permanents made it look like a bush in need of pruning.

I was not an athlete as a child or teen. I grew up before girls had sports teams or competitive anything that involved running, throwing, or jumping. By the time I was a young adult in my 20s and 30s, I realized how much I had missed by not being physically active. To make up for lost time, I tried and failed at tennis and golf. I began running with a friend; I explored women's exercise groups, like yoga, Jazzercise, and Pilates. It felt good to stretch my muscles and work up a sweat. The more active I was, the stronger and leaner my body became. I felt invincible, just like Wonder Woman. But then type 1 diabetes, adult onset, knocked the wind out of me. My weight dipped into an unhealthy range and I was exhausted all the time, and stressed when my blood sugars rose or fell to dangerous levels. I was depressed. My mind and body crumbled under the weight of diabetes until I learned how to live with it.

It has taken me years to know this body and what it is capable of, to learn how it holds pain and joy, and to understand the extent of its physical weakness and power. Now that I am well into my seventies, I see my body morphing again. It's starting to break down, just like an old car in need of repair. My back hurts a little more, I tire more easily, and I'm fretting over a sagging chin, fleshier deltoids, and freckles that have grown into large brown spots. But this outward manifestation of who I am really doesn't matter anymore. I'm ready to embrace and love my body with all its warts and imperfections. I believe my gray hair and wrinkles reflect wisdom hard won from raising two sons, experiencing the ups and downs of a long marriage, enduring disappointments, and mourning the loss of friends. Each smile line and furrowed brow is a testament to a story that has enriched my life. I know this body won't last forever. Still, it is the only one I have. It has walked a thousand miles with me and will eventually see me home, my constant friend and companion.

Every Pore

CINDY ATLEE

They tell you it's okay, now.
You can finally be comfortable in your own skin.
They say you have been around
enough.

You are wise
enough.
You have earned the right not to care what other people think of you.
You can move as yourself, now.

But they don't mean it.

They say these things as your skin becomes
crepey, splotched, blue-veined.
As if that skin has a fleece lining on the inside that
holds you, keeps you safe, makes you brave.
They say the outside doesn't matter anymore.

But they don't believe it.

Because the other thing they tell you is,
change everything.
Push away what you've earned the right to call your own.
Alter it, instead, replace whatever isn't smooth.
Become more like porcelain, like glass, again,
risk the cracks in that.

Tighten, too, and lift. Soften rough edges.
Dull what's become sharp, angled, protruding.
Do. Not. Be. Brittle.

But they are wrong.

This much is true:
You know who you are.
You are not bound by skin.
Not breakable, now. Not glass, but mirror.
You are spirit, stardust, smoke. Like light
at the edge of twilight.

Draw that to you.
Open every pore.

The Crone Questions the Stereotype

BETTY JO MIDDLETON

Could wisdom really come with age,
regardless of one's circumstance,
or might one stay completely clueless,
none the wiser through the years,
experience teaching nothing much?

When I Am Old and Inconvenient

BARBARA LEARY

When I am old and inconvenient,
maybe I'll go where I am driven
maybe I'll accept what I am given.

      Probably not

When I am inconvenient and old,
there are three states of being
I don't wish to be in:
      house guest
      house pet
      house plant.

Conveniently, I am a once and future flight risk
skilled in the art of departure:
      smile compliantly
      wait for the nurse to leave
      pull out my own IV
      slap on a bandage
      slip on my clothes
      slide out the door
         Paul Simon singing in my ear.

When the going gets dicey
before they take away my license
maybe I'll keep a bag packed for a final adventure.
      A case of fine wine, some righteous weed,

and off I'll go
Westward Ho!
Imagine
        me in the desert
        groovin' on peyote
        pals with a coyote
        cozy with an old cowboy
        of a mind to build a fire, tell an old woman a story.
Maybe I'll write a new story.

        Probably not

When I am old and insufferable,
beloved child of mine,
imagining open roads
still
you'll weight me here, dear:
dearer than freedom.

I won't take what is mine but not mine to take.
I'll go while my going is good
and leave
my rest
to Fate.

Woman Wild

SHANNON PLUMMER

If you really knew me, you would not try to name me.
If you really knew me, you would feel my words.
If you really knew me, you would hear my body.
If you really knew me, you would taste my desires.
If you really knew me, you would celebrate my flavors.
If you really knew me, you would smell my mistakes.
If you really knew me, you would challenge my grace.
If you really knew me, you would shatter my image.
If you really knew me, you would see my heart.

If you really knew me, you would not try to name me.
Because when you do, you dissolve my magic.
When you do, you tame my wild.

Writing

Writing Prompt

SHAILEEN BACKMAN

Write the day—the early morning peek through window blind slats at neighbors waiting at the bus stop. Little girls in tights sit cross-legged on the cold pavement while moms crane their necks for a glimpse of yellow.

Write the silence of the post office lobby that you have entered countless times, the padding of your feet, the smell of paper.

Write the pleasure of choice in the grocery store aisles, with no one needing you, calling, or texting.

Write the mail scattered across the dining room table, strewn and unsorted, and keys jumbled in the small basket hanging from the doorknob.

Write the whistling flute of the mourning doves' tail feathers as they flutter away whenever you creak open the back door.

Write the drying wishbones sitting in the small dish on the kitchen windowsill, just above the sink. You wonder what to wish for, hope you'll win, then remember it means the other will lose.

Write the smell of hot dust on cast iron radiators, the hiss and clank of the first heat of late autumn.

Write the softness of your husband's newly shaven face and the faded scent of soap.

Write the almonds soaking in milky brown water waiting to be slipped from their skins and ground into milk for your fifth cup of tea.

Write the orange sky and the silhouetted black tree as you close the blinds once again, and once again.

The Life of a Writer

VALERIE BURTON

It's like the life of anyone else:
You wake up, have coffee, read a book
And think, one day I will write something this good, actually better

I'll change lives with my words, make readers marvel
Today, it'll be so great to spend some time with my writing
To hone my craft, get words on a page, edit, create

First though, you'll go exercise so you can be all set with that
After showering off the sweat and making more coffee,
It'll be the perfect time to write

Oh yeah, you forgot you wanted to go to the farmer's market
Returning those library books was also on the list
So get those taken care of, then come home and write

An unexpected text inviting you to get a pedicure?
You have been neglecting your feet, not to mention your sexy sandals
Poor things languishing in a dark closet all summer

So 3:00 is perfect, gives you just enough time to have a bite of lunch
Just not quite enough to start writing
I mean, what if you get all into it, then have to leave?

That nail place, you forgot, is right next to Cooper's Hawk
It's a little early in the day for wine, but happy hour started at 4:00
So we should not miss out on those half-price bottles and appetizers

You hardly ever see Allyson, so it's a great time to catch up
And when you get home in the evening, you'll go write to the desk
Ha ha, of course you mean right to the desk

Over your third glass of bubbly white wine, maybe you'll talk about
How much you enjoy writing stories and poems
And how it's so hard, but oh so rewarding, being a writer

At home the couch waits with open arms, so you stretch out
The desk beckons, a meek attempt from across the room
What about me? it whispers, guessing the answer

Don't you understand? you sigh
I have been running around all day, and I'm tired
How can I apply my brain when it's floating in a sea of half-price wine?

But I should, shouldn't I?
I want to, don't I?
I want to write. I'm a writer

But right now, I'm just glad you're my writing
And not a puppy I have to take outside
If you could pee in the house, you'd have the upper hand here

Listen, I promise we'll hang out tomorrow
I have a lot of time, it'll be great
And I swear I won't let the life of a writer keep me from my writing

Erassurance

MARION SHEAFFER

Sugared Pansy Pink:
the color of an eraser
on a Dixon Ticonderoga

Pencil, #2
to be
exact.

Comforting
cajoling
convincing

suggesting an easy fix:
wipe out mistakes,
start over again.

No commitment,
no risk:
like dating

not marrying,
like renting
not buying,

offering reassurance
and resilience to this
reticent writer.

One Word at a Time

BARBARA GALVIN

With the touch of a single key, every word she had labored over was gone. No SAVE button in case of doubt. Just DELETE. Months of work wiped out in a single tap. Months of agonizing rewrites obliterated. Georgia was done, determined never to write again.

Seven months earlier, she had begun brainstorming. It started with one light bulb moment, and she soon began filling her notebook with ideas. She people-watched and created characters. She went for walks and settings took root. She listened to conversations and dialogue emerged. She was on fire, unstoppable, ready to start her novel.

Now, after months of rewrites going nowhere, characters becoming boring, plots lacking any substance, she trashed it all and went back to her old job at the public library—a job she had given up to focus on her writing. Here she once again surrounded herself with the treasured authors she so foolishly thought she could emulate.

Georgia quickly settled back into her old routine. On one particularly slow day, as she set out to straighten the shelves, she thought she heard a tiny whisper like a puff of sweet air escaping from between two books she had just rearranged on the "A" shelf. She drew closer and leaned her ear toward the books but heard nothing.

"Such foolishness," she mumbled. "Books don't whisper." And she moved on to the "B's." All was quiet.

Unable to shake the feeling that she was being drawn into something, she returned the next day to listen closely. The A and B authors were silent as she passed by, but when she reached the "C's," the whisper returned, more pronounced and insistent, forcing her to stop.

"This is nuts," Georgia exclaimed, loud enough to cause a collective SHHHH from the library patrons. But drawn in by a gentle wisp of honeyed breath, she leaned closer.

BEGIN

That was all.

Georgia wrote down the word in the notebook she still carried around with her from her days of writing. She bent closer for another listen, but the books were quiet. They had said all they were going to say for that day.

Eager now to return to the stacks, Georgia waited each day for another word. And one at a time, they obliged.

BEGIN

AGAIN

OBSERVE

LISTEN

WRITE

Georgia continued to write them down, her curiosity piqued.

As weeks passed, she strained to listen but heard nothing. Then one day the pattern changed. This time, instead of a whisper, she found a scrap of paper lying on the floor between the shelves. On it was written a simple word, a name: JOSHUA. Puzzled, but no longer surprised at the strange turn of events, she tucked it into her pocket and brought it home.

All was quiet for a time after that, and Georgia accepted that this might be the end of her word collection. But during that time, she turned the name Joshua around in her head, spoke it aloud, and wrote it over and over in her book until she began to "see" him. He was tall, with dark hair and brilliant blue eyes. He dressed in jeans and hoodies and carried a backpack with the name of a school on it that she could not decipher.

Soon after Joshua was clear in her mind, another word drifted off a shelf she was organizing. This word was a place: UNIVERSITY. Georgia placed this one in her pocket as well, and on her drive home she began to notice buildings she had not paid much attention to. As she considered them, a clear picture of a campus emerged. And immediately she saw Joshua standing at the entrance to one of the buildings.

Back at the library, entire sentences began littering the floor. Georgia saw bits of dialogue, most not making any sense until she had collected enough of them to construct a conversation. Knowing that a conversation required more than one person, Georgia created a female character named Angie to talk to Joshua.

In the evenings, she was consumed with thoughts of Angie and Joshua. Crises emerged and more characters were fleshed out. And when she was stymied, Georgia returned to the whispering shelves and dropped words for inspiration.

Years later, when she was a bestselling author, Georgia was often asked, "Where do you come up with your ideas and your characters?"

"I go to the library, and I always seem to find just the right words," she answered with a twinkle in her eye.

In Fifty Words or Less

BETTY JO MIDDLETON

64

A lot of words on paper
may not make much sense.
They could be only random thoughts,
with verbiage quite dense,
a writer's futile efforts
to fill another page,
to find some words that want to soar
and free them from their cage.

This Poem

BARBARA LEARY

This poem has a mind of its own.
It storms in without knocking, wind-wild and muddy
Drinks milk from the carton
Slouches in the good chair
Squints at me sideways
Rifles through my things
Takes what it wants and leaves the rest strewn around the room
Wakes early and starts the coffee
Collects the eggs from the chicken coop,
then disappears without warning.

This poem has a mind of its own.
We drink, we argue, we gossip
We daydream
We stare at the blinking cursor in companionable silence
You first, it says.
No, you.

A Buzzing

CHERYL JOHNSON

In the rug I see
the dry bed
a stream trickles through.

The electric cord
snaked under the desk
a sweet potato vine.

Salmon petunias spill
over the chartreuse vase
in a courtyard in bloom.

The dogwood spreads
wings in the noon sun's
embrace of leaves.

Chartreuse, mandarin
morning indigo
a snapshot of the soul.

A snotty fly
tickets the window,
manic suicide.

Can the blue basket be
God, blackberry pie?
Does the morning taste?

My green eyes
harbor hellebore's
melancholy arks.

The fly at the window
pauses, honoring
death's itch.

A poet is a fisher,
her bait the depth
words take.

Without Metaphor
SUMMER HARDINGE

tomorrow we will meet the horses/ after they have run the fields
cantered around us /nudged / this is not a war poem/

we use soft ropes/ drape shoulders and withers/ coax them in/ they
will not halter for this/ is not a war poem/

a drink some oats / a comb and brush-out/ the day will be warm/
they will blink in the sun/

watch/ a patch of clover swarmed with bees—they will not/ be stung
this is not/ a war poem/

we rub in circles/ loosen roughness dust flies—not a war poem/
we'll lean-in to each other/ flank to flank/ but not in a war poem/

we will speak of harness/ rein/ stall shook and break/ but / not
spoken as war poem/ we will turn/ look

for hatch/ ladder/ the release the catch/ in this not-war poem/ and
wrap/ arms /around necks/ as if it / could be otherwise /

Letter From My Mother

MARY AXIOTIS

Dearest Mary,

Do you remember when you came to Greece one summer and asked me about my life story? Do you remember what I told you? I said, "I don't want my dirty laundry to be published for everyone to know." I hope that comment didn't discourage you from writing it, but I think it did.

Well, I'm telling you now that you should write my story. Yes, you heard me right. You should write my story, and don't waste any time telling it. It will be good for my granddaughters and great-grandchildren to know who I am, even though they don't know me well. It's good for them to know their history. You are so far away from anything Greek, and so disconnected from Greek history, customs, and traditions, that you need to write this story.

If you write my story, they will be able to learn a bit of Greek history, and the reason Greeks lived in Turkey. They will also learn how Greeks migrated back to Greece under the Greek and Turkish governments' population exchange agreement set by the Treaty of Lausanne in 1923. Many Orthodox Greeks were victims of the genocide that happened prior to the exchange and during the Greco-Turkish war. Many, including my family, lost all their possessions when they were forced out of Turkey in the 1920s with only the clothes on their backs. So much had happened to them. So much blood was spilled and so many lives lost. My family and I were fortunate to survive.

You will have to write down the way my father died, even though I am not quite sure I know the real story, either. No one wanted to talk about his death. I was told two different stories about it. One was that he committed suicide when he lost his jewelry business in the fire that the Turks started in the nearby Armenian village. The other one was that he died from a stroke when his business was burned to the ground. Both versions have substance, but you decide, Mary, which one you want to use. Pick one and write about it.

You will also have to write about my Uncle George. If it wasn't for him, I don't think my mother, with three young children, would have been able to survive. He helped us settle in the city of Thessaloniki, and took us in until we found a place to live. He was always there for us. You remember, I always went to visit him and his family. They lived close by. You visited them too, when you were young, quite often. Do you remember that, Mary?

Oh, and don't forget to write about my sister. She left this world at such a young age. She was so good to me. She insisted I get an education, and she was the one who paid for my studies in clothing design in Athens. I know I didn't talk about her much because the pain was too strong. But you can write about her, and how nice she was to me. She worked in the tobacco factory with your grandmother. She contracted tuberculosis, and by the time she was diagnosed it was too late. Don't omit her from the story.

Don't forget, Mary. Write my story. And of course, you must write about your father and how we met. Remember what I told you, that we met at a wedding? You will have to write of the time he served in Egypt with the English during War World II. You have the leather album that he brought back with him, with all the pictures that he took. I assume the album is in your hands. You remember that album, Mary, don't you? We used to look through it during the winter months waiting for your father to come home from work.

You have plenty of material to fill up a book. So, Mary, sit down and write it before it's too late.

Your loving mamá,
Anna

Longings

Dreams of …
MELANIE HUGHES

Love is boundless
    connecting, in ties
        that don't bind,

weaving bodies like tapestry,
    seeking the mastery
        of trust.

Trust in the other
    who now must
        wonder

at gifts that unfold
    pleasures untold
        in bliss.

A breast at thy lips
    waits soft tender
        kiss,

dreaming unceasing
    of reverent
        caress.

Memories of the future
    sweep over me,
        under me,

a vision
     that yearns
          for boundless love.

I Saw Love

CHELA HARDY

I saw Love in the window of a quaint shop at the end of a road I'd often passed but had never ventured down before. Its beauty was breathtaking, and I found myself staring at it in amazement, mesmerized, unable to turn away. I wondered how it felt to the touch. I wondered why I'd never been this close to it before. I wondered if I could make it mine.

I had to try, and I had to do so immediately, for surely such a rare and precious gem would be snatched up quickly. Heart pounding and pulse racing, I hurried inside, tightly clutching my handbag—though fully aware that nothing inside held enough value to purchase this particular item. Love would not be bought with mere coins or printed paper. It was worth far, far more.

"Can I help you?" asked the shopkeeper as I entered. I stepped forward eagerly, but the voice that responded was not my own. It came from somewhere behind me, and I knew even before I turned that I was too late…again.

"I'll take that item. The one in the window there," said a woman standing off in the corner. I hadn't seen her when I'd entered.

"Shall I wrap it?" asked the shopkeeper, but he'd barely come from behind the counter before the woman had snatched Love from the display window and tossed it into a worn, tattered shopping bag. I watched with grief as it settled at the bottom of the bag, buried beneath items of far less value and far less beauty.

"No," she replied curtly, stepping past me and dropping the bag to the floor with a crash as she faced the shopkeeper who, with clear disgust at her indelicate treatment of Love, returned to his place behind the counter to complete their transaction.

She was gone a moment later, swinging the bag with such force that its contents shifted. The shopkeeper turned sympathetic eyes to me as I watched her go.

"Can I help you?" he asked gently, but he already knew he could not. "Miss," he said as I turned to leave. His hands disappeared beneath the counter, then quickly reappeared holding a white gift box wrapped in lavender ribbon.

"Can I offer you Hope?" he asked, setting the box at the edge of the counter.

With tears in my eyes, I shook my head and reached out to gently pat his hand.

"Thank you," I said with the widest smile I could manage, "but I had that once and I've since given it up."

The air seemed cooler and the sky darker as I stepped outside the quaint shop at the end of the road I'd often passed but had never ventured down before. I took one last look around me and sighed, knowing I'd never make the trip again.

Unrequited
LISA COLBURN

The dented aluminum billycan sways
on a tripod of sticks over snapping tongues of fire.
Sparks spray into surrounding dark.
Soon there will be tea.

Across a sweep of rust-red sand, village lights glow,
fairy-like, in a blanket of star-pricked darkness.
No sound except wind rustle, fire crackle,
three voices hushed in desert silence.

The ranger sits beside me on a low outcropping,
arm slung over my shoulder, pointing to Virgo.
They call her the virgin, he murmurs, breath singeing my ear,
but her legs are open. The stone on which we sit is warm.

My friend wants him, body angled, leaning with desire.
He wants me, signals sent in dark eyes, brush of hands. But

I want no one.

Just this place. This time.
These billion trillion stars.

A Yellow Hue

EMILY DILLON

His bedroom was a large upstairs space in an old Victorian. A house with white walls, crown molding, and wood floors, the Victorian had been repurposed as a commune, its grand front porch strewn with cracked string instruments and hammocks. In his room, the majesty of the 1920s gave way to piles of boy clothes and the smell of a radiator. I dropped my backpack on a clothes heap near one of two twin beds. He had invited me to stay at his place for the night and I'd take the second bed, happy for a reprieve from my own roommates.

And also, well, I liked to visit him.

I don't remember if we went to bed at the same time that night (was this the night we all stayed up passing around the guitar, or the night that we crept upstairs early, exhausted from dinner conversation?) but I do know that at some point I was awake and he was sleeping.

Sleeping near him had happened before. In college, I had camped in the same tent with him and his girlfriend, and fallen asleep on his futon in the dorms. This, however, a few years later, was the only time that I can remember sleeping with just us there, just our breathing, for the full night. I remember the soft sound of the fan, the small wind of his breath. I remember a yellow hue that probably meant it was morning. He had olive skin and the light made him look tender as I peeked across the room from the second bed.

Why am I noticing his body?

I looked at the outline of his back through the morning fuzziness—even with no glasses, I could trace every muscle—and instinctively knew the answer that I didn't want to admit: I wanted to be over there with him, next to him, in him.

In another story, I slowly get up and slide the sheet down to my feet. I put my toes down onto the cold wooden floor and do the thing that I always wanted—I walk toward him, stepping over t-shirts and boxers and socks and sweaters, and then, without thinking, because it is only natural, I slip in behind him and put my chin in his neck. He wakes up just enough to know that what would always happen is here, reaches around to find my hand and brings it over his waist. He goes back to sleep. I smile and close my eyes, to finally rest.

But this isn't that story.

Instead, I turn back to the wall and the next time we sleep in the same house, I find a room with only one bed, not two. I had lied to myself that I could sleep next to him without wanting to sleep with him. It was one of many lies to keep him near.

Disillusionment at Ten O'Clock

KATHLEEN BARRY-RODGERS

dedicated to the Beatles, April 10, 1970

Christ, you know it ain't easy
to wake up in the morning
and hear that Walt Whitman committed suicide
before he finished Song of Myself.
He left a note we hoped would say more than
you've been such a lovely audience, but go home now.

      Something inside screamed then
      more than the ear can hold
      though it was not nearly filled.

I wish you wouldn't do this, how can you
your love-loss is mine too, don't do it
it really doesn't matter who's wrong or right
your colours are primary, are permanent

and paint me. Please
please me

The Ship of Her Body

BARBARA FARMER

after "Rhapsody for Healing" by Sandra Crouch

In the ship of her body, a storm of great magnitude
enters as the brain erupts, spreading volcanic ash
deep into the right side, along the gyri and grooves of sulci.
A harbinger.

Treatment to excise and stage
the volcano fails. Weakness advances
to loss of leg, arm, hand
on her dominant side.

Anger, fear, and bargaining enter
and reveal a person torn
of treatment, torn of civility,
torn of expectancy.

Steroidal flare-ups erupt
and project onto loved ones.
Her body hovers into dependency,
pain, immobility.

The ship of her body
calls out for time,
time to go on.
The body is listening.

Forever Waters

MARLIS MCCOLLUM

I once stood tall and scanned my white horizon.
King.
I once walked miles on frozen tundra.
Strong.
I once tasted the blood-salt of my prey,
felt the rush of life into my limbs.

Now I swim and swim and swim
in withering fatigue,
teeth, tongue, and belly wailing
to taste flesh.
I long to rest,
to sleep in the white,
but there is only darkness,
only softness to push against
again and again.

I am not made for these forever waters,
this clawing chill,
this pulling grasp.
Ice, ice, land, land, where are you?
I long for a hard bed to rest my darkening head.

My strength eludes me.
My size betrays me.
My limbs grow weak in wasting.
Sleep is the enemy, sleep is the friend.

It wins.

My legend is now a whispered memory,
my tribe an abandoned people,
my crown a fallen relic,
as forever waters take me down.

My Room of My Own

PAMELA G. SCHMIDT

During the housing bubble of 2011, we lost our home. A family of five with two dogs, a cat, pet snakes, and geckos, we finally found and rented a small farm. I lost a lot of indoor space, but gained four stalls and a tack room, all of which were very helpful for the critters to come. Nature abhors a vacuum, especially with two 4H kids and one horse-crazed teenager in the family.

But I lost my quilting room, the one place in my old house where no one was allowed without my say so. No way for my husband to drop off a shirt that needed a button, or a pair of pants needing a hem: "I've already turned them up – just whenever you can get to them."

My quilting room was a place where everything had a place. Especially me. I had painted it a light purple color, and filled the walls with inspirational quotes, postcards from friends, and creative ideas. It was a very feminine space, with no unused tables or chairs where someone might drop down with a computer or a guitar: "Just for a few minutes Mom – I just need someplace quiet for a few minutes (hours, days). You don't mind, do you?"

In our old house, I didn't even need to shut the glassed French doors, as everyone knew not to cross from the hardwood floor onto the white carpet without being invited. From the windows looking out front to the street, I could hide when I saw neighbors coming to visit, letting them think I was out on a walk with the kids. My young next-door neighbor told me that when she was babysitting across the street she never felt alone, because she could see the lights on in my quilting room and knew that I was there, close, creating something beautiful.

I didn't always sew or create in there. I dreamt, too, often while looking at a quilt on the wall. Thinking about how the colors blended or didn't, and wondering why I found such joy cutting up perfectly good pieces of cloth into little pieces, only to sew them back together in a new way. The dreaming would come as I followed a path of stitching, wondering if anyone would notice the words hidden in the rhythm of my needle. I dreamt of whom the quilt would belong to. I rarely started with a plan or design in mind, or a need to coordinate with someone's bedroom rug. Eventually the owner would show up and the quilt would find its new home. Then I would clean up my quilting room, sorting out the scraps by color, cleaning the lint from the sewing machine's crevices, and oiling the hardworking joints that kept the whole operation moving.

In this new house, I make do in the dining room. While I know our horses won't come knocking at the front door, Tico, the huge red foundling, has a way of standing patiently at the water trough, which I can see from the dining room windows. I lose my path among the colors to wonder when the water trough was last filled. And because there are no doors on this dining room turned quilting room, mending seems to pile up on the empty desk space I had cleared for color ideas and mixing fabric palettes. The grays and khakis of my husband's neatly turned-up pants seem to suck the colors out of the room, taking my creativity and soul with them.

The family printer is in this usurped dining room too, next to the piano that fits nowhere else in this smaller house with homeschooled children. Apparently, waiting for the printer's output awakens a long-forgotten need to practice the piano. The same song, over and over, interrupts the soothing whirring of my well-oiled sewing machine, and reminds me to check the time and go start dinner.

A room of my own is the loss I mourn the most. I can deal with the clutter dumped on the kitchen counter, the guitar, mandolin, and ukulele cases left open on chairs and couches, the muddy boots in the entryway to the backyard, where we now have chickens. I don't even mind how those backyard chickens peck on the glass panes in the door that leads into the kitchen, peering in to see what we are doing and turning their heads, obviously wondering why they can't come in to our fascinating and cluttered kitchen. But a mom, a woman, needs a space of her own.

A space where no one can dump their papers, or plop down on the one chair that is only empty because I am up searching for the perfect piece of fabric.

I've considered the stalls. But where would the 4H animals go? Nature seems to abhor a vacuum, except in a woman's soul.

No Place Like Home

VALERIE BURTON

You don't like your sandwich?" Mrs. Chesterton asks her husband, seeing him grimace as he drops his lunch to his plate.

Mr. Chesterton shakes his head. What's to like about this tossed-together excuse for a meal—thick, unwieldy slices of processed turkey unevenly stacked between two pieces of bland white bread, a slab of orange cheese hanging out the side. Something similar might be found in the lunchbox of a kindergartner left to make a sandwich without supervision.

Other residents seem to be consuming the sandwich—or the gloppy Swedish meatball option—without despair. The food at the assisted living facility they'd moved into several months ago at the insistence of their son and daughter isn't always this bad. But the utterly careless presentation of the sandwich gives Mr. Chesterton a sharp pang of longing for his own kitchen that is intensified by the belief that he's been duped.

When they'd toured Bluebird Manor, the first thing the director said was, "All of our employees are dedicated to making the atmosphere as home-like as possible for our residents." Brochures touted "lovingly prepared meals created fresh for you every day by Chef Michael, using local, healthful ingredients." What poppycock.

It was true that Bluebird Manor was closer to the kids and offered amenities such as a pool, fitness center, social hours, and day trips. "Anything to keep your mind off the fact that you're moving into an old-folks home," Mr. Chesterton had joked during their tour. His daughter had flashed him a scowl as she walked ahead, holding her mother's arm.

And so he bit his tongue when the director enthusiastically described how they'd just screened *The Wizard of Oz* in the full-size movie theater, complete with popcorn. Picturing his own life being blown away by a tornado, Mr. Chesterton wished his daughter would understand that no matter what was offered, it would make no difference to his wife if they moved here or to a tent in the woods. He, on the other hand, had to say goodbye to his barber, his golf buddies, his library card, his lawn mower, his coffee shop.

Prior to moving, he and his wife had shared a spacious condominium with a sunny, glassed-in porch where he enjoyed his newspaper and coffee every morning. But their kids expressed increasing concern about their mother's erratic behavior (putting keys in the refrigerator, leaving food cooking on the stove until the smoke alarms went off), insisting her dementia was a ticking time bomb.

When Mr. Chesterton fell and hit his head on the bathroom sink and Mrs. Chesterton did not respond to his calls for help because she was on the porch tinkering with her plants, his daughter raised the alarm. "You shouldn't have had to crawl to the phone in the living room! Not to mention those blood stains on the carpet are going to be hell to clean when you finally let us sell this place."

Mr. Chesterton wasn't concerned about the bloody carpet, but the emergency room visit to stitch up the gash on his head dissipated his fortitude to fend off the kids. He believed their promises that they'd be able to "help with Mom" if they lived a little closer.

He'd had to do the packing. Mrs. Chesterton inevitably took more things out of boxes than she put in, sometimes infuriating him by undoing his painstaking work. "Would you please just leave the boxes alone?" he'd snap, then he'd feel guilty. Her brain's decay wasn't her fault, he knew that, and it was only his heart's vow of 56 years—"Till death do us part"—that quelled his anguish about uprooting their lives.

Janice, the rotund, zealous activities director, now swoops to their table for afternoon recruiting. "I hope you're both enjoying lunch," she trills. Mr. Chesterton is about to point out his sad sandwich, but she has already moved on from concern about their meal. "Can we count on your beautiful voice at our sing-along this afternoon, Mrs. Chesterton?"

Beaming up at Janice, Mrs. Chesterton reaches out for her hand and says, "Of course, dear!"

"Wonderful! And I hope we will see some of your lovely family at the ice cream social after?"

Mrs. Chesterton, still smiling, says, "Oh yes, I do believe so."

"Bless your heart," Janice gushes, sailing away to the next table and leaving Mr. Chesterton vexed by his wife's belief that the kids will visit.

Once they had helped get the boxes and what furniture could fit into the one-bedroom suite that was their parents' new home, their son and daughter approached subsequent visits with an escape plan. "We have a game to get to," or "We'll be gone before Bingo, we know Mom loves it!" they'd insist, as if they didn't want the grandkids to inhale too much of the assisted living's air.

Mr. Chesterton looks at his wife, completely engrossed in taking another bite of her sandwich, and envies her ability to look forward to the afternoon he dreads. Mrs. Chesterton has never asked about the condo, if it has sold, where they are. It's as if there had been no life before Bluebird Manor. She will smile throughout the ice cream social whether their children are there or not.

Why can't I? Mr. Chesterton thinks. Despite his better judgment, he hopes that maybe, just maybe, this will be the day the kids decide to show up and take them out to dinner, or to one of the grandkids' games—anywhere besides the stifling library with the shelves lined with fake books and a cheery volunteer chirping, "Would you like vanilla or chocolate today?"

Most likely, though, he and his wife will end up back in the dining room at 4:30 for another round of Chef Michael's creations. Mrs. Chesterton, as always, will heartily enjoy her food after a joyful afternoon belting out show tunes from the past. And Mr. Chesterton, as always, taking his seat across from his wife, will dare to dream that he too may find pleasure in the options on the menu.

Jasper

BARBARA ROTH

The wind sends leaves sailing
and swirling through the air today
Their muted colors of burnished
copper and amber reminding me
of autumn days when he walked beside me,
tail wagging, ears cocked forward,
eager to explore.
Memories of coming home
to find him in his perfect sit, waiting
on the edge of the rug for me to greet him.
On days like this my heart feels his absence.
I look around corners hoping he will be there,
will leap into my arms. Instead I am left
only with his shadow and a photo of him
in the last light of the day.

All That Talk About Chickens

LISA COLBURN

for Duane

The last time we spoke
we argued about chickens.

We are nineteen.
I clench the phone
booth receiver, your voice
tinny in my ear. Over
and over again I say,
"You bought *chickens?*"

You want:
a dusty plot of farmland;
chickens pecking in dirt;
John Deere squatting in the field;
the sweet smell of cow shit hanging in the air.
I do not.

But I also do not want:
your lobster boat aflame, sinking;
your body hauled up
from the indifferent Atlantic;
your mother, brothers, sisters, shattered
on the shore of loss; me,

wishing I could take back
all that talk about chickens.

Prayer at Night, Passing the Taxidermy Shop

JOANNE LOZAR GLENN

after "Grief" by Matthew Dickman

The deer's eyes stare from inside the dark storefront
as my father and I walk by, our shadows fuzzy
under the street lamps. It's October, almost Halloween,
and wind flicks embers from my father's cigarette.
We are hunting colored leaves. We will iron them
between waxed sheets, mount them like paintings
in black paper frames. And Miss Malik will call it Art.

All these years later the smell of Marlboros
summons up that night and the one after,
when my father left us with the taxidermist's
wife to have supper so he could sit a wake.
I forgave him leaving us to her care while deer
watched like conscripted sentries below her kitchen.
I forgave her the gruel that made us retch. But not

his getting cancer, the hard words that shielded,
then silenced, what I couldn't voice: can I be forgiven
for taking all these years to count myself lucky
just because the moon was full and darkness
wrapped around us like a blanket, just because
one night I passed a taxidermy shop gathering leaves,
holding my father's hand?

MayBelle Goes to an Estate Sale

AMY LYLES WILSON

The dream came over the weekend, the one with her dead mother in it. MayBelle hasn't dreamed about her mother often in the six years since her death, although MayBelle frequently senses her mother's spirit with her. And certainly she feels her mother's influence, even lives it out. On separate occasions just last week, MayBelle quoted her mother to a friend, heeded a piece of advice delivered decades ago, and missed her with such fierceness that she had to step outside a restaurant to collect herself.

Maybe MayBelle will make that her goal, "collecting herself." She will gather up the pieces she's lost hold of, the ones she either thought didn't matter or was told didn't count. She'll root around for her childhood dreams and begin to honor those goals she let fall by the wayside. She'll walk as far as she has to, searching for the just-right shards and fragments. Hers.

Along the way, MayBelle will have to put down some things, she realizes, for one middle-aged goober can't carry it all. She'll start with that pesky self-doubt and the tendency to see herself through a distorted lens. Then she'll move on to a constant need for approval and an everlasting internal refrain of: "You are not doing enough." She'll get rid of clothes that don't suit and accessories she doesn't need. (Why in the world did MayBelle buy that mustard-colored tunic?) Out with the affectations that never did the trick anyway, and say goodbye to being unduly influenced by every piece of advice—sought or otherwise—that comes her way.

As she hunts and gathers and sets aside, MayBelle will focus on collecting what counts and what connects. All she cares about and all she can offer. Those dreams, people, and activities she can tend and nurture well. She hopes she will need a big basket to hold it all.

In the dream, MayBelle's mother is happy. She is not worried or anxious. She is not scared of the dementia that garbles her memories, or the death that looms. Instead, she is laughing merrily with one of her precious great-grandchildren, a young girl with a big bow in her hair who pushes MayBelle's mother in a wheelchair. They are both smiling, big toothy grins, as they loop round and round. They exhibit such joy that MayBelle chooses to believe it is more than a dream. It is the stuff of life.

MayBelle doesn't usually cry about her deceased parents on those days you might consider made for mourning: death anniversaries, family birthdays, major holidays. Most likely she begins to cry, or is forced to her knees, at unpredictable times and in unexpected places. Like this weekend, when she went to an estate sale, the kind where it's obvious someone has left the house for good, as opposed to a garage sale intended to make room for more stuff. What's left is what's left behind, after the inhabitant has died or moved to a retirement community or skilled nursing facility, perhaps. For some reason, in her mother's final days, MayBelle much preferred "skilled nursing facility" over "nursing home." She was choosing her words deliberately, she surmises, so that she might survive the fact that her mother could no longer care for herself in a meaningful way.

MayBelle knows the territory because she's been there, deciding what stays in the family, what gets donated or sold, what needs to be discarded. How to choose between a memory and a brass candlestick? Indeed.

As she made her way through the tidy townhouse, MayBelle looked for old postcards and photographs, small things she might use as writing prompts or for her art projects. Exiting a bedroom she glanced in the closet, where she noticed clothes like her mother wore in her later years: matching, machine washable, sturdy with a hint of style. MayBelle began to weep, seeing the same brands she and her sisters used to buy for their mother, clinging to any last gesture they might offer her when so much had been taken away. For a while there, MayBelle could tell any woman of a certain era where to get the best deals on Alfred Dunner and high-waisted cotton underwear.

MayBelle is what's known as a "highly sensitive person"—yes, it's a thing—and she can be moved to despair at warp speed. Bless her heart. She is also a person with an estate sale problem. Probably she should not spend so much time rummaging around in the pasts of strangers, as it often makes her sad and she does not need one more tea towel. But this weekend it is where MayBelle found herself, wondering what had happened to the homeowner (was it a happy life?), forking over eleven dollars, and missing her mother.

The Missing Button

SHAILEEN BACKMAN

It was a nice shirt, some designer brand, maybe J. Crew or Ralph Lauren. The point being that he seemed well taken care of. But he wasn't. He wore his grief like a secret shroud to protect himself from others. It had been a whole year, and still the pain cut deep and was seemingly fresh. It was right there under the surface, and he limited his exposure lest it spill out too easily. A nervous laugh, a glance askance, a ducked head as he entered and made his quick exit. Demure. Deferential.

He stayed home a lot. Home was safe, though lonely. It was both haven and mausoleum. No TV on, because they didn't like most television shows. When they were they.

The things she left were still in place one year later. He confessed that it took him six months to change the sheets on the bed she died in. He didn't know what you were supposed to do. And there on the floor near the bed were the little drops of lotion he had used to soothe her aching hands and feet. Crystallized. It hurt to see them. But he couldn't erase them. He couldn't do that. Not yet. He told me all this while wincing, but no tears. The tears were kept at home, in the dark of the silent night.

I had been a grief counselor for over a year, so none of this was new to me. I recalled the lady who slept with her husband's ashes, in their wooden box, on the bed "where he belonged," and the widow who kissed the leftover hair in her husband's hairbrush every morning. Pain. Longing. Clinging to the last little tangible things, the personal and intimate ones. Not ready to let go.

I was no stranger to grief, but this one somehow crept in with a new discordant twang. Maybe because he was my age. But also because of that one button.

Educated, quietly eloquent, physically fit enough to play hours of tennis. Allusions of vibrancy juxtaposed with rumpled cotton. I wanted to lean over and gently button his shirt for him, but of course I could never. It was too personal, too intimate. Even to mention it would be akin to treating him as a small child, which he was not. It was a dilemma for my maternal instincts. Loud, that button. It struck like a black piano chord.

He came back three weeks later to talk again, same shirt. The one he saved for appointments. Same unbuttoned button, right there in the middle. And if he shifted in the chair, as he did in his established discomfort, a gap would form. I had to avert my eyes. Not my place.

What is this? I asked myself. *What is this?* Not just the button, but my reaction. And it occurred to me that it was not unbuttoned after all, but missing. And he at 57 had no wife to sew it on for him. Not a failure of dress, just loss—reeking, bleeding, messy loss. The hundredth story of my work this year, and yet somehow new. Stinging.

It didn't matter. It was just a button. Just me making up some explanation. Maybe it was always missing. Maybe it came that way. Maybe he set it aside in the small dish atop his dresser, next to the sentimental knickknacks of vacations, and her photograph. Probably not. Maybe he knew how to sew, but didn't want to. Or he didn't notice, didn't care. It was low on the list. It was inconsequential.

The part of me that mixed over-helpfulness with compulsion wished I could pull out the miniature sewing kit I kept in my desk drawer, because once I was a Girl Scout leader. I could gently say, "This will just take a minute." And set things right. But I couldn't fix any of it, or make it pretty, or whole. Professional boundaries. Personal boundaries. Respect. All I could do was nod kindly, listen, find some soothing words, and hold the space for him, the space where he could say the things the others no longer knew still weighed on his heart. Nobody else knew the depth of his distress, the depth of his need to honor her. Nobody asked anymore. It had been a year.

Reverence

Missing Piece

CHERYL JOHNSON

March, in the herb bed, shrunk pods
Of cayenne, a collapsed apple, rotted plums.
This is the circle I fill.
Add twigs, cured leaves,
Grass like an old woman's hair.
In the chives a few still-green stalks.
Time all around them.
Spring is an old woman.
Skin crepe, hands a wrinkled map.
I place a forget-me-not in the bed's heart.

Dangling

MARTHA J. PADGETTE

It dangled there
    Helpless
Out of reach, black wings extended
    Hanging
From the large tree behind the house

It dangled there
    I couldn't help
Call the arborist they said
    Or the fire department

No, neither, I realized would reach him in time

Helpless, I watched
    And fought to decide
Knowing in my heart
    His time was passing quickly

Mournful, I offered
    Energy and love
Yearning to soothe
    And ease his suffering in some way

Hopeful, I called
    Asking the birds to return
To assist in any way possible
    To snip the string that held him helpless

Or simply to be with him as he passed
        Majestically with ease and grace
Into the great beyond
        Towards the kiss of dark clouds blooming

Because it was clear there was really nothing more I could do

And so they came
        The two
Acknowledging
        Showing they were there for him

Coming so close and almost landing
        Then realizing it was beyond them as well
They circled . . .
        With recognition and reverence

Then were gone
        Flying slowly towards the coming storm
Into the restless wind
        They vanished

And I was released
We all were released

Each dangling no more

Anything But Common
CHERYL SADOWSKI

This morning I watched
a gray house spider
who watched me
(I am sure of it)

wave my watering wand
over shrubs and rails
casting a lustrous mist
upon her diaphanous home

she approached one droplet
grasped by feathery tarsus
and plunged into the center
of its watery sphere

like a child with cherry pie
anything but common.

Ants Are Beings, Too

LORRAINE BURTON

I have never been a huge insect lover, but I've also never liked killing them. I attribute this partly to squeamishness and partly to a reverence for all living beings that I only fully became aware of once I stopped eating animals. It took me a while to get to a fully plant-based diet and lifestyle, but ultimately I felt that if I couldn't kill an animal myself or bear to watch another human being slaughter or commit other acts of cruelty against the cows, chickens, and other sentient beings caught in the meat and dairy industries, then I should not be partaking of their flesh, milk, or eggs.

So although I could not articulate even to myself the existential guilt that washed over me on the occasions when it seemed I had no choice but to squash an arthropod invading my living space, I already did my best before embracing veganism not to kill bugs. My eventual commitment to not knowingly contribute to the suffering or death of any animal made me see the hypocrisy of killing a wayward spider simply because its life path had led it to the corner of my living room, and I doubled down on my efforts to relocate rather than exterminate indoor insect intruders. But sometimes I still wondered whether I was taking this veganism thing too far. Did I really need to capture the yearly spring influx of ants one by one and release them into their natural habitat?

Then one day, as I was about to push an ant from the edge of my cat's water bowl into the dedicated plastic container I use to catch bugs, I hesitated. I don't know what made me stop and look at the ant perched on the rim of the bowl. Maybe it was her own moment of stillness before carrying on with her day, not yet aware of me or the danger I might present. From her perch on the edge of the bowl, this ant leaned in to take a drink of water, then lifted her head and wiped an antenna with one of her front legs, perhaps a post-imbibement ritual as she decided what to do next.

In that moment of looking at an ant up close for probably the first time in my life rather than mindlessly scrambling after a scurrying pest who had it in for me and my home, I saw another living creature taking a drink and contemplating her next move. Okay, perhaps that is a bit too much anthropomorphizing, but I did connect with that ant on an existential level, seeing us as two individuals living the lives we'd been given, doing the best we could, going about our business in an effort to survive and thrive. How could I end the life of this fellow being in the midst of her dharmic path? As the karma of it all hit me, I understood in that instant that no, I wasn't taking things too far.

I resumed the process of scooping up my friend and her buddies and carrying them outside that day, and I continue to do this with as many of her relations who stop by as possible. I try to remember to look at some of them and say hello before saying *adios* as I release them into the garden. I realize that in doing so I may in fact be changing their fate, that these tiny critters may be faced with death and destruction from human feet, weather, or other perils they would not have faced in my home. But don't they *want* to be outside? Am I changing their dharma or leading them back to their true path?

I can't think too hard about all that or I would never leave my house. But I can cherish this encounter, which felt like a communion with the universe and all the creatures in it, no single one more or less deserving to go about its business with the right to life, liberty, and the pursuit of happiness—and perhaps a drink of water along the way.

Union

LAUREN RUTTEN

> *"I dedicate all thought to union."*

This reminder appears on my iPhone at 9 a.m. every morning. I sit on my Grandma Helen's rickety old metal chair with the pull-out steps. The step chair enables me to reach the flour and sugar on the top shelf of the cupboard. I lean back against the cold tile wall when the reminder flashes. Whenever I want to distract myself with social media or emails, this message appears as the activation button is pushed.

> *"I dedicate all thought to union."*

What is this statement, from Marie Perron's *A Course of Love*, really asking of me? Dictionary.com offered me these definitions, which seem quite obvious:

Union - noun
1. the act of uniting two or more things.
2. the state of being united.
3. the process or result of merging or integration of disjoined, severed, or fractured elements, as the healing of a wound or broken bone.
4. the junction or location at which the merging process has taken place.

Thesaurus.com brought me closer to the concept I am engaged with daily:

Synonym study
1. Union, unity agree in referring to a oneness, either created by putting together, or by being undivided.

Union has 45 synonyms to consider as alternates. Join or merge seem readily interchangeable, but would they change the meaning of this lesson I am practicing? I was never much of a joiner, and merging onto highways is always a challenge, but maybe this experiment will be enlightening.

❧

8:00 a.m., last Wednesday. I am the white frost coating the invasive weeds, garlic mustard and ground ivy, at the head of the driveway. The sun has not yet reached the right edge of the property where my car is parked. I am millions of water molecules suspended in delicate fractal forms. Later, I will disappear in the warming air.

Beyond the railroad tracks glaring white hot, beyond the old winding road leading out of town, tucked between ridges of bare hillsides, I am a blanket of white fog spanning a quarter mile. Find me where warm meets cool, night meets day, in a place called condensation. How many mornings have you chased me up and down the narrow roads in hope of taking my photograph, only to be foiled by my elusiveness?

I rose early with the sun, drifting up Hill Street with the promise of catching a glimpse of myself hanging low against the French Broad. Where Hill Street and Skyway Drive meet, the fields fall away in layer upon layer of fading grass coated in frost. Far off is Staritt Mountain, where I have tucked myself into the northern face.

My dog Asa and I walk a narrow gravel path around Blannahassett Island, avoiding deep rutted mud puddles left after five consecutive days of rain. F150s and Foresters parked in the grass at last week's art festival formed these impressions. Mufflers don't appear to be a requirement around these mountains. My father, Harry, used to sit in his big white rattan chair on the front porch hollering, "Jesus Christ" and a string of obscenities in the direction of any loud vehicle driving past our house. Along with the Norfolk Southern train horn blaring day or night, engines of old clunkers and diesel trucks make the house and his old bones rattle.

Asa doesn't hear much of anything these days. Used to howl every time the train whistle blew. Doesn't even turn his head now. Can't hear my whistle or voice calling to hurry up. Used to practically catch a fox, squirrel or a dozen grazing deer as we hiked in Manassas Battlefields. Off lead he'd go flying through waist-tall grass, chasing whatever caught his attention. The white tip of his tail the only thing I could keep my sight on. Last Sunday, the bright white tail of a doe waved across a field on Mulberry Gap Farm. Asa would have loved a good chase, but he hasn't much run in him anymore.

A small tuft of white fur rests on the living room carpet, half a foot from Asa's bed. The soft clump, like a baby's ringlet, perhaps scratched off in a fitful night's sleep. Asa's white hairs merge with the red oriental rug, the first big purchase made at 24 and newly wed. Deep in the fibers with the ones long gone, James and Ginger, Buddha, Mango and Clementine, Rosie, Tuesday, Kitty Kitty, and my first dog, Mr Wili. Three inches of white fur, soothing between my fingers as I grab hold. I am the cotton ball shoved in the pocket of old jeans, no need to tell anyone what I'm here for. Don't resist being little, the comfort of something soft rubbed against the upper lip. White cotton fibers embedded with lint, bits of pencil or cookie. Two fingers gently tease apart a thin wisp of graying white fluff.

"I dedicate all thought to union."

I don't remember the first time I left. Maybe it was kindergarten. The time the puddle was there. The rows of miniature desks and small wooden chairs. I lied. Told her it wasn't mine. The puddle said it was. And the pants with the wet splotch running the distance from crotch down pant leg toward the floor. And some other girl's pants, the ones I wore home. And the bag with the wet ones hidden from Mommy. The pants, shoved down the laundry chute into the basement, falling into darkness and a basket of dirty white sheets. Or maybe stuffed in the back of the dresser drawer, far enough back where no one would find them. Where the next time they'd be dry.

Maybe I left the first time the puddle was there in the morning, on the sheets of the big-girl bed. The white antique iron bed Mommy bought for me. The sheets, covered with the blanket, so no one would know.

Maybe the first time I left was when the baby arrived. Before I turned two. Middle of January. Sent outside to play. In a snowsuit. Next thing my mother hears are my howling screams. Clothes thrown off. Standing naked. Turning red. *"Wait til your father gets home,"* is all she said.

Now I can't wait to leave his room. The scent of urine a one-two punch of memory and repulsion. My father needs a shower and clean gown. He hasn't left the hospital bed of his own volition for nearly two weeks. Help will be here soon but not soon enough. A plastic urinal with an inch of dark yellow piss hangs from the bed rail. Accidents happen. Someone will clean him and the sheets up after I leave.

❧

7:21 a.m., Tuesday. As the window shade is opened, an unexpected white coating on the leaves outside the window says good morning. The bitter cold smacks my face as Asa and I walk along the gray gravel, flanked by a dusting of fresh white snow. Across the river from the tip of the island, a small white house stands in stark contrast to the hillside of bare trees. This is the confluence, where two avenues of the river merge back to a single flow of the northbound French Broad. They say it's one of the world's oldest rivers, pre-dated only by the Nile and the New River.

"I dedicate all thought to union."

Off lead, Asa sniffs every blade of grass, withering weed, and fallen leaf to mark the perfect spot with his pee. Let the world know, I am here. Standing at the far edge of the island. Slowing my breath. Here on the rush of white-capped river, crossing to the distant shore. Here inside the small white house. Looking out the window. Greeting myself, good morning.

Branches

LISA FISCHER

When the frost shimmers on last year's garden and the birds ride the naked branches in the cold wind, I will think of you. I will remember the time we hiked down through the woods to the river, the frigid air seeping through our jackets and pants. How we carefully made our way to the river's edge over the hardened mud, our boots slipping on patches of ice. We stood together and watched the frozen chunks move slowly along like flotsam and jetsam from some faraway ruined land. How I watched your small, determined fingers pry rocks from the frozen bank and then fling them out, staring intently as they disappeared one after another down into the water's secret depths. I will remember everything, and the memory will wash through me like an emotion. Then the cardinal's red body will remind me again of today. And the soft gray and tan of the mourning doves in the snow will move in my heart with love. And the frozen water droplets will hang from the shepherd's hook and reflect the world in tiny, beautiful mirrors.

Soeur de Mon Âme

MAGGIE BUTLER

Returning to Dublin that December
I thought what an odd year it had been,
not at all what I'd imagined, and then
I thought of you.

It wasn't the year you'd planned, either,
even though I'd given you a calendar
to fill the future squares of your days
with plans and hope.

Those last two weeks were damp and raw;
granite-gray Irish winter days when evening
begins just at dawn's end, and I needed the fire
to keep me warm through those hours

we shared on the phone, and my tears transformed
the lights on the tree into stars, and when,
even under such heartbreaking weight,
the elegant alchemy of our friendship continued
to hold that sacred space where we'd shared and received
the unedited versions of our writing and ourselves.

You were leaving.

Each day you drifted further away, but still, still,
still, you sought that space. When you could no longer speak,
and Andrew's voice, thin as hare soup, told me
it will be soon,

my spirit, my strongest connection to you,
knew it was true.

So I let you go,

lighting a candle for the path you had to travel alone
until you found every beautiful thought
and sentence ever expressed and written,
every person you'd ever loved,
all the dogs and cats you'd nursed and nuzzled,
every childhood memory made perfect,
and I hoped, for your sake,
God Himself.

For Dorothy Molloy Carpenter
1942 – 2004

Night Sky, Chichen Itza

SOPHIA ELBERTI

with a grateful nod to Wordsworth

Wordlessly, we climb single-file
to the rooftop. Circular stairs end
and bend us in reverence toward
the night sky, a dazzling mirror
of infinite jewels.
One star, topaz blue, calls to me;
I watch, then turn away,
the intimacy too much.
My eyes wander, but go back,
the attraction too much.

This star speaks to me of you
and I wonder *Is that you
in that heavenly body?*
With this floating thought
you are beside me…

I know then
the fullness of you.

It is a brief visit, but enough.

My Day to Die

BECKY BOLT

If I live to become an old woman, I hope to spend my last days in a place that now exists only in my imagination. It is a place where the world is perfect because I have realized my perfection. It is a place where there is complete joy because everyone there lives in love. It is a place of connection and harmony with the earth. It is heaven.

The land is large and beautiful. There are lush fields of flowers and thick forests full of mystery. Mountains can be seen in the distance, and they send their cool, clear streams winding down to us. The music of the water is magic. All of creation shares this land. The plants blossom and animals thrive in an atmosphere of unity. We are one. Each sunrise and each sunset is a reminder of God's unending desire for us to be happy. At night, no light other than the stars and moon is visible, and that is enough. Even when the weather is cold or wet or stormy, it is a celebration of nature's excellence.

The people who live with me in this place are my sisters. They are women who have spent their lives serving others and discovering the God within themselves. Like me, they have come to this place to enjoy their last days in peace and in preparation for whatever lies ahead. There is no fear, no suspicion, no worry. There is trust and confirmation. We are God's children, working together for ourselves, each other, and our world.

We live in small cabins, either alone or with others. The cabins are simple, but very comfortable. There is a fireplace and a screened porch set up for sleeping on pleasant nights. There are more windows than walls, and each cabin has a view of sunrise and sunset. At this point in our lives, we know that less stuff is more, and that the really important things cannot be owned.

At the heart of the land are two beautiful stone buildings sitting next to a stream. They are in a shallow valley and can be seen from the cabins perched on the surrounding hills. Inside one building is a kitchen and dining room where we share meals, a library with a collection of books that rivals any public institution, a music room full of instruments, and a health facility for exercise and healing. Just outside is a huge garden where most of our food is grown.

The other building is circular with a stunning chapel in the center. The ceiling of the chapel is stained glass that makes the sunlight dance on everyone who enters. Several rooms encircle the chapel. There is a prayer room where someone is praying every minute of every day. There are classrooms, individual rooms dedicated to studying and honoring many religions, and rooms for silent meditation. These two buildings are the hub of our community, and they stand on holy ground. The very air and light surrounding them vibrates with Spirit.

Every woman joyfully helps the community run smoothly by doing those tasks that make her heart sing. Some cook, some clean, some garden, some teach, some heal others. My contribution is to share the secrets of the wild animals living with us on the land. Most of my sisters do not know the secrets, but understand and respect the sacredness of wild things. They come to me with questions, searching for their connection with all of God's creation: What bird sings that song? Where do the snakes sleep at night? Why does the mother turtle not care for her young? I take them through the fields, past the streams, and into the forest, and we watch the world unfold. I am the interpreter, clearing away misunderstanding and fear, replacing it with love and wonder at the magnificence of our Garden of Eden. And every day I, too, am reminded, am renewed, and stand in awe.

Now I am an old woman. I can no longer lead my sisters to the forest, so they carry me. We sit beneath the trees and listen to the frogs tell us of the coming rain. This evening, my sisters will not carry me home. It is my day to die. They will pat my hands and kiss my cheeks and leave me where I belong. The earth will be warm on my back and the breeze will caress my face. I will slip away, guided by the cry of the screech owl and the light of a billion stars. Tonight in the chapel, there will be songs of joy.

Where I'm From

REBECCA WHITECOTTON

after George Ella Lyon

I am from starlight and angel dust,
celestial feathers floating on the breath of All That Is.
I am from the dark of space
and the center of first light.

 I am from the molten core of earth,
glowing, flowing to the surface,
oozing toward the ocean,
where it is quenched, hardened into form.

I am from acorns and sunflower seeds,
and from vines spreading life through leafy tendrils.
I am from birch and maple, sycamore and oak,
rooted in power, swaying with the wind.
I am from rocks and rain, stone and sand.

I am from gazelle and tortoise,
from shark and minnow,
bluebird and eagle.
I am from the mother bear who nurtures her cubs,
and the vulture who feeds on the dead.

I am from compassion of saints
and mistakes of sinners.
I am from the love of mothers
and anger that drives worlds to war.

I am from joy and sadness,
pleasure and pain,
life and death.

I am from All That Is
and all that ever will be.

I AM.

Unfolding

JESSICA WILSON

A slant of light awakens the scene with brilliant strokes.
An accordion of spare, sharp delineations —
pine, stone wall, jeweled pond in a bezel of iris and boxwood.

Moments later the sun adds a few more strokes.
A prism of cobwebs laced with dew
widens the delicate lens of morning.

Folds unfurled, the brilliant shards have
claimed their place on the checkerboard.
Light and shadow are equal partners now.

As sure as the rooster's call,
what's lost to the day will bring
new revelations tomorrow.

Appendix: Writing Prompts

Almost half of the pieces in *Unfolding* were written in response to prompts—mostly in Market Street Writers workshops, but also in workshops led by Summer Hardinge, Sonya Huber, and Pat Schneider. A writing prompt can be anything: a suggestion, quote, overheard bit of dialogue, object, image, video, piece of music, or—quite often—a poem. The prompts below follow the order of their creative offspring, and the poems can be found online. Perhaps one of these will spark your own creative fire!

Origins

- "Soft Thunder" by Jake Skeets (*Gulf Coast Morning*)
- "The Theft Outright" by Heid E. Erdrich (*Before the People Came*)
- Write about a childhood game (*Life on the Farm*)
- Write about the quality of light (*Pastures*)
- "Where I'm From" by George Ella Lyon (*Where I'm From*)

Herstory

- Close your eyes and imagine a summer evening (*Elegy*)
- Make a list of things you're grateful for and pick one to write about (*2,000 Albums*)
- Write about a pair of glasses (*Reading Glasses*)
- Write in response to a photograph, beginning with this phrase: "In this one, you are . . ." (*Metamorphosis*)
- "Skins" by Freddy Macdonald (video on melissameierart.com) (*Every Pore*)
- Girl, Woman, Crone (*The Crone Questions the Stereotype*)
- Write about your "wild nature" (*Woman Wild*)

Writing

- "don't forget to write" by Maya Stein (*Writing Prompt*)
- Paint chip in "Sugared Pansy Pink" (*Erassurance*)
- Think about one object you interacted with today and write the whole story (*A Buzzing*)
- Write an unsent letter (*Letter From My Mother*)

Longings

- Make a list of everything you want to write about, then pick one (*A Yellow Hue*)
- "Rhapsody for Healing" by Sandra Crouch (*The Ship of Her Body*)
- "Grief" by Matthew Dickman (*Prayer at Night, Passing the Taxidermy Shop*)

Reverence

- List or free write, using sensory details, all that has happened to you this day so far (*Missing Piece*)
- Write about an insect encounter (*Ants Are Beings, Too*)
- "Ask Me" by William Stafford (*Branches*)
- "Where I'm From" by George Ella Lyon (*Where I'm From*)

Gratitude

One morning, after I gave a writer friend an update on the progress of this anthology and some workshops in the pipeline, she remarked, "You've built a beautiful life for yourself, all around writing." I felt the truth of this immediately. Writing has been a passion of mine since childhood, but it's the community of writers I belong to that fills my spirit with joy. We've so often heard that writing is a lonely pursuit, and it certainly can be. But when we come together to write and share our stories, we feel buoyed, energized, and fortified to do our work.

My first gratitude goes to the late Pat Schneider, founder of Amherst Writers & Artists (AWA). I am doing the work I love because of the writing workshop method she developed and shared with so many. I give thanks for Pat each time I begin a new writing circle.

Six of my AWA colleagues appear in *Unfolding*, and I am grateful to each of them as well. Maggie Butler and Sue McCollum were my first AWA workshop leaders and mentors, and I deeply appreciate their unfailing friendship and encouragement. Summer Hardinge (along with Maggie Butler) helped select and revise some of the poems, and writing in her workshops is always a pleasure. Amy Lyles Wilson generously shared her experience of creating the Pilgrim Writers anthology, and she has been a cheerleader for this project. Joanne Lozar Glenn is a wise, gentle friend whose perspective and example I appreciate. Lauren Rutten is a gifted photographer and artist who contributed the image for the cover. I am blessed by their friendship.

When virtual assistant Chela Hardy of AskChela volunteered her services for the anthology, I had no idea how she could help. Then I learned to appreciate administrative support! Many thanks to Chela and to John Dillon of the Dillon Law Group for advice on the publication contract. I also appreciate Rebecca Whitecotton for sharing her publishing and marketing expertise, and Lorraine Burton, Joanne Lozar Glenn, Christine Koubek, and Sue McCollum for their editorial assistance.

Becky Bolt, Barb Galvin, Lynn Hays, and Pamela Schmidt also provided proofreading support. It takes a village!

The following anthology contributors made generous financial donations to help defray design and printing costs: Lynn Hays, Shayne Johnson, Yolonda Nicely, Shaileen Backman, Tina McCoy, Lorraine Burton, Valerie Burton, Martha Padgette, Barb Galvin, Barbara Farmer, Sue McCollum, Barbara Leary, Jessica Wilson, and Diana Read. Thank you! I'm also grateful for the support of my husband, Dave Colburn, who brightens my days with his warmth and good humor.

Finally, I'd like to thank all the writers who have participated in Market Street Writers workshops, classes, retreats, and creativity coaching sessions, whether for a season or a decade. Your words, your stories, matter. I am honored to know you.

Contributors

Cindy Atlee is a writer, artist, and coach who uses words to paint pictures and images to tell stories. After a 30+ year career as a branding consultant, she's now focused on helping people make imaginative, expressive connections to self, source, and others.

Mary Axiotis' travel writing has appeared on the Greek government's tourism website (www.visitgreece.gr) and on the Chios Island government's tourism website (www.chios.gr/en/). Her photography has been featured in *The Ultimate Gardener*.

Shaileen Backman is a Licensed Clinical Social Worker who double majored in English as an undergrad and enjoys writing essays, journaling, participating in writing workshops, and weaving. At the end of her career, she worked for Hospice as a Bereavement Counselor and is currently writing a book on grief.

Kathleen Barry-Rodgers is from Brooklyn, New York. After receiving her Master of Arts in Teaching Secondary English at Trinity College, she embarked on a much loved 40-year teaching career, from which she is now retired. She still loves reading and writing, and would go back to school tomorrow!

Becky Bolt is a retired wildlife ecologist who has authored or co-authored over 40 scientific publications. She joined a creative writing group in 2003, where she learned to write from her heart. In 2021 she published a book for beginning bird watchers, and she currently facilitates emotional breakthrough writing groups.

Lorraine Burton is a book and magazine publishing professional and freelance editor/copy editor. She is also a yoga teacher helping folks counteract the effects of a sedentary lifestyle and serving on the board of the Yoga Teachers Association of the Hudson Valley. She and her husband split their time between Ossining, New York, and Philadelphia, Pennsylvania.

Valerie Burton is a social worker who advocates for animal welfare and education in Guatemala when she's not writing or watching tennis. She started writing stories at a young age and particularly enjoys flash fiction and graphic novels.

Maggie Butler is a retired psychotherapist, writer, and painter who lives in Western Massachusetts and Ireland. As an award-winning writer and former certified Amherst Writers & Artists workshop facilitator, Maggie has led creative writing workshops and retreats in the U.S. and Ireland for many years. Her work has appeared in numerous literary journals.

Lisa Colburn, founder of Market Street Writers, offers Amherst Writers & Artists workshops, journaling classes, and creativity coaching in Leesburg, Virginia. Her poems, essays, and articles have appeared in *Peregrine, Washingtonian, The Washington Post*, and various Unity publications, among others. National parks, independent bookstores, and writing circles are her favorite places.

Maxine Composto, Master of Human Relations, Certified Bereavement Specialist, and retired government Administrative Officer, is pursuing her love of learning and passion for writing. She won first place for flash fiction in Word Weavers' 2024 Writing Contest. When she is not writing, she is crocheting baby beanies for a hospital.

Emily Dillon is a writer and educator from Maryland whose creative work ranges from nonfiction to poetry and all the lyrical places in between. An avid reader, she also publishes book reviews and teaching guides. Currently she is an Assistant Teaching Professor in the Writing Department at Loyola University Maryland.

Sophia Elberti is a retired government worker residing in Northern Virginia.

Barbara Farmer has written with Market Street Writers for 10 years. Born in Queens, New York, much of her writing focuses on her childhood in a diverse neighborhood. After a successful 38-year career as a Registered Nurse, she moved from Northern Virginia to Sarasota, Florida. She has two wonderful children and two beloved grandchildren.

Lisa Fischer has lived in Loudoun County, Virginia, for the past 30 years. In her free time, she enjoys writing, gardening, reading, and the outdoors.

Barbara Galvin has been writing short pieces in workshops for years and published her first novel, *Kaleidoscope*, in 2020. She is now concentrating on flash fiction and short stories. She lives in Leesburg, Virginia, with her husband of 54 years. She has three children and seven grandchildren.

Joanne Lozar Glenn is a freelance writer, editor, educator, and writing retreat leader whose work has been published in *Beautiful Things* (River Teeth), *Peregrine*, *Brevity*, and other print and online journals. Her most recent book, co-authored with five other writers, is *Memoir Your Way: Tell Your Story Through Writing, Recipes, Quilts, Graphic Novels, and More*.

Summer Hardinge lives near the Potomac River. A former high school teacher, she leads Amherst Writers & Artists workshops in the Washington, D.C., area. Her poetry appears in *Beltway Poetry Quarterly*, *Peregrine*, *Stonecoast Review*, *Literary Mama*, and other print and online journals. Summer is happiest when swimming or gardening.

Chela Hardy is a longtime Virtual Assistant and the owner of AskChela LLC. Author of *Noted! Business Lessons Learned from Twenty-Two Years of Virtual Assistance* and *Become a More Confident Virtual Assistant*, Chela blogs about her industry at AskChela.com and teaches related sessions as a Loudoun County Public Schools Adult Ed instructor.

Lynn Hays is the former owner of HAYSMAR, Inc., a boutique research and communications practice. Now retired, Lynn enjoys writing, reading, and volunteer work. She is a long-time Jupiter, Florida, resident and a widow with two grandchildren in Virginia.

Melanie Hughes is a sporadic writer of songs and poems, both serious and humorous. She is a four-season gardener and chicken-loving nature freak who loves healthy cooking and sharing her creations with friends. As a career, she teaches vision-impaired people independence skills and loves her job still, after 27 years.

Cheryl Johnson, Emerita University of Idaho, English Department, lives in Lewiston, Idaho. She is the author of *From the Country of Home: A Remembrance; Multiple Genres, Multiple Voices: Teaching Argument in Composition and Literature;* and co-editor of *Come to the Table: Recipes for Loving and Serving.*

Shayne Johnson lives in Purcellville, Virginia. She has joined Market Street Writers in a variety of writing workshops both online and in person since 2019. She is an avid reader and writes a monthly newsletter on Substack called "Shayne's Bookish News."

Christine Koubek's stories have appeared in *The Washington Post, Poets & Writers,* and *Chautauqua,* among others. Her work has received awards from the American Society of Journalists and Authors and an Elizabeth George Foundation grant. She holds an MFA in Creative Writing and loves working with writers to help shape their stories.

Barbara Leary writes short fiction, poetry, creative nonfiction, and children's books, one of which—*The Climbing Tree*—won first place in a *Writer's Digest* competition. Her work has been performed on public radio and has appeared in magazines, newspapers, and online. She teaches graduate-level writing courses at Georgetown University.

Marlis McCollum is a professional writer whose articles have appeared in a variety of publications, covering topics as diverse as art, religion, aviation, and technology. She is also a published poet, an artist, and a Kundalini yoga instructor. In her poetic expressions, she often finds inspiration in the natural world.

Susan Ives McCollum is an Amherst Writers & Artists affiliate and certified legacy writing facilitator who has led workshops in Malawi, Africa, and Northern Virginia. She is the co-author with Diane Hartingh Price of *Write Your Stress Away: Tame the Tension in Your Life*. She is currently focusing on legacy writing as a path to health and well-being.

Tina McCoy started writing in 2009 using Julia Cameron's *The Artist's Way Morning Pages Journal*. In 2019 she completed a 90-day book writing challenge, and she is currently working on a memoir. She is also an accomplished artist who has taught adult art classes through the Fairfax County, Virginia, Recreation Department.

Betty Jo Middleton has been writing poetry for several years, after a long hiatus. In addition to her two chapbooks, *Senior Moments: Poems* and *Second Fifties: Poems*, her work has been published on Alexandria, Virginia's DASH buses and in several anthologies. She has received poetry prizes from the Poetry Roundtable of Arkansas and the Arizona State Poetry Society.

Yolonda Nicely began writing seriously when she retired from the Smithsonian Associates and joined the Osher Lifelong Learning Institute

(OLLI) of George Mason University in Fairfax, Virginia. Since then her work has been published in the OLLI magazine, and she continues to write memories, short stories, and poems.

Martha J. Padgette retired from a career in IT and now enjoys avidly observing nature and exploring the craft of writing. She wrote several sections of the book *No One Path: Perspectives on Leadership* (Women in Technology, 2009). "Dangling" is her first published poem.

Shannon Plummer has at her fingertips, lightning; in her voice, thunder; and within her presence, the earth. She is a powerhouse intentional creation coach, shamanic practitioner, artist, speaker, author, and singer wrapped in a divine package. Her approach combines practical, spiritual, shamanic, and metaphysical wisdom.

Mary Quattro is a retired social worker, real estate paralegal, and certified retreat leader. She is blessed with a son, grandson, dear friends, and good neighbors.

Diana Read began writing at age eight, as editor and sole reporter for a neighborhood newspaper titled *Freedom and Torment*. After retiring from a career in marketing communications, she has written short stories, blogs, novels, and novellas. Lately she has begun writing and acting in plays.

Barbara Roth has enjoyed expressing herself through writing since childhood. Her poems have appeared in various literary journals over the years, and she also has a published chapbook, *Stepping Back*. Much of her inspiration comes from the time she spends outside hiking and photographing nature while accompanied by her husband and dog.

Lauren Rutten is an artist and writer living in Marshall, North Carolina. For 11 years, she accompanied her husband along his cancer journey until his passing in December 2021. Her work explores the subjects of loss, remembrance, longing, and connection as she examines the intersection of body and spirit.

Cheryl Sadowski writes about art, books, landscape, and nature. Her writing appears in *Vita Poetica, After the Art, The Bluebird Word, About Place Journal, The Orchards Poetry Journal, EcoTheo Review,* and *Bay to Ocean Journal.* Cheryl lives in Great Falls, Virginia, where she works as a communications consultant.

Pamela G. Schmidt loves to learn, create, and teach. She made her first dress at age 10, and ever since she has considered needles and threads her dearest friends. She has used them to build community with 4H groups, a quilters' co-op in Malawi, and anyone who asks, "what are you making?"

Marion Sheaffer has enjoyed a long teaching career where she has worked to spark a love of reading and writing in her young students. In her free time, she likes to read, journal, sing, play guitar, and write songs.

Robin Sofge is a Library Branch Manager in Northern Virginia who was formerly a community reporter and obituary writer. A traveler, she is currently trying to learn Italian on Duolingo in hopes of traveling to the Ligurian Sea in Italy. Her happiest adventures have been with her family.

Laura Sturza is a writer/teacher living in Rockville, Maryland. Her work is published in *The Washington Post, The LA Times, The Boston Globe, Lunch Ticket, AARP's The Girlfriend,* and *Shondaland,* among others. She is completing a memoir, *Better Late: Adventures of a Midlife First-time Wife.*

Rebecca Whitecotton is an introspective writer and mixed media artist inspired by nature, meditation, and the malleability of quantum reality. Her book, *Pull Your Self Together: A True Story of Alternate Realities, Spiritual Healing, and Dimensional Wholeness,* was seeded in a Market Street Writers retreat.

Amy Lyles Wilson believes it's the sharing of our stories that saves us. As a writer, story coach, and spiritual director, she helps people tell the stories they're called to tell. Her work has appeared in a variety of publications, as well as on National Public Radio.

Jessica Wilson grew up in a world of words and images. After a career in publications and print design, she took up the brush and the pen. The natural world provides her with the poetic moments she aims to capture in painting and in verse.